"The journey of a thousand miles begins with a single step."
—Lao Tzu

SPARK!

A Heart Centered Journey of Growth, Reflection and Unleashing Your Warrior Soul

GALE NIENHUIS

Illustrated by Kayla Schweisberger

Copyright ©2023 Gale Nienhuis

Published in the United States by Spark Media
www.mysparkjourney.com

All rights reserved. No part of this publication may be reproduced, distributed, or transmitted in any form or by any means, including photocopying, recording, or other electronic or mechanical methods, without the prior written permission of the publisher, except as permitted by U.S. copyright law. For permission requests, contact the publisher at mysparkjourney@gmail.com

The statements, circumstances and individuals in this book are fictional and for the purpose of explanation. The broad categories of circumstance and symptomatology that many people have experienced are presented as a learning tool for the reader. Always seek the advice of your physician or other qualified health care providers with any medical or mental health questions or conditions you may have. If you are in need of medical or mental health care or treatment, contact your medical or mental health provider. This is not intended as treatment or in place of mental health treatment.

ISBN 979-8-9880485-0-3 (Paperback Editon)
ISBN 979-8-9880485-1-0 (Spiral Bound Edition)
ISBN 979-8-9880485-2-7 (eBook Edition)

First Paperback Edition: August 2023

Book Design by Angela Grace
Illustrated by Kayla Sweissberger
Edited by Aaron Bubis
Cover Image by Klassic Designs

To my dad, Earl, for always being understanding even though he may not always understand the latest happening. To Jared for being the most awesome, patient, nephew ever and making all things technical happen. To Stephanie for always saying "how's the book coming," taking pictures in the snow, and all the love and support. To Mark and Sydney Hanrahan for having eagle eyes, good ideas, and taking good pictures. To Ryan Hanrahan for answering difficult questions and helping with scary parts. To my dear friend Diane Nickless for reading really rough drafts, clinical consultation, and for all the incredible enthusiasm. To Anna Quist for encouraging me to never give up. To Gwen for having so much knowledge and being willing to share it. To Aaron Bubis for hanging in there to Guatemala and back and to Kayla for being brilliant and open. To Angela for being willing to step in at the last minute, being incredibly organized, patient and knowing all things! To Thea for helping me realize I could write a book.

Table of Contents

The Beginning 9

Your Tool Kit 25

Self-Love 45

Journey to Connection 69

Warrior Soul 83

North Star 103

The Spark Wrap Up 119

Resources 125

1
The Beginning

Things to Think About

Love and care for yourself—no matter what!

Rely on your own voice and trust yourself.

Make decisions in your life based on self-love, self-honoring, and strength.

HELLO AND WELCOME

Star fragments of the universe! I'm so excited you are here. C'mon in, sit down, grab a cup of something you love, and let's get started. I am going to be your guide.

This is a reflective journaling workbook focused on building personal resilience, moving into yourself, and rescuing yourself from doubt, fear, anxiety, and uncertainty. Instead of being held back by those feelings, this book guides you to discover and move into your true self . . . your SPARK!

This book will help you build an authentic life based on self-love, self-care, and true self-understanding.

I've been a seeker all my life. With my curiosity, appetite for knowledge, and endless yearning to deepen my connection with myself, I have traveled a road with lots of twists and turns. Along the way I've found beauty, wisdom, and divinity in expected and unexpected places. I've developed a path of self-discovery that I have shared with others and now I would like to share it with you.

WHO THE HECK AM I?

My name is Gale, and I am a therapist, journaler, art materials junkie, animal rescuer, spiritual seeker, book lover, and a whole bunch of other "intersections" that make me who I am and no one else.

I've worked in the mental health field as a clinical social worker for many years, and prior to that I was an occupational therapy assistant and behavioral health technician. My calling has always been to help people who are struggling. I've done this work in my own private practice, schools, community living spaces, shelters, and hospital psychiatric units. Through these experiences, I've had the great fortune to work with lots of women on their path towards something different in their life.

It is with a great sense of honor that I have done inspiring work with amazing, evolving women to find their true selves. We have worked through struggles with uncertainty, built up confidence in ourselves, learned self-love, and many of the other pieces that go along with finding and honoring your genuine self. We all struggle with these difficulties, but it helps to build yourself a roadmap to self-discovery and that's what I'm here to help you do! Within these pages I've created a place to explore your dreams, strengths, values, obstacles, creativity, and joy.

My work has brought such joy, inspiration, and reflection to myself and the women I've worked with over the years. I've realized the tremendous importance of learning who you are and to navigate your life in a way that is supportive and nurturing to your true self: your spark!

SPARK! is a journaling workbook designed to help and support you in figuring out what you want out of your time on this planet.

WHY IS THIS SO IMPORTANT?

Within all of us there is a core uniqueness, an essence unlike anyone else. This is your spark! Use this workbook to unearth that spark within you. Explore it, learn about it, and decide what it is you want to do with it. Your values, beliefs, intelligence, kindness, creativity, and uniqueness are all things that make up your unrepeatable, individual, spark. It's who you are.

Each human being is a precious piece of gold in the treasure chest that is this vast universe we are all a part of.

STARTING ON THE PATH

We all grew up with caregivers of some sort who shaped, guided, and instructed us in ways both nurturing and destructive. Now it's time to take that information and decide what will help you on your soul journey. Are you where you thought you would be? Are you where you want to be? Life, particularly in the United States, comes at a frantic pace. We're not always sure how we got to this moment!

WHAT I'VE LEARNED

What I've learned through my work, and just being a human on this planet, is that so many of us don't start the work because there are too many other crazy things sweeping us along through life. You start school, work, a family, a career, and on and on, with no time to take a breath. It's important to take time as you grow and change to figure out what your goals, dreams, beliefs, wants, and needs are. Finding your precious spark can start right here.

FINDING YOUR IMPORTANT QUESTIONS

Who are you? What do you value? What brings you great joy? What do you struggle with? You will continually ask and investigate these questions as we move through this book.

We are about to embark on a fantastical, soulful, creative trek into the known and, more importantly, the unknown.

In this first chapter I will explain all the pieces and parts of this book.

WHAT THIS BOOK OFFERS YOU

This book is an interactive space where YOU pick your journey and your pace: a place where you can think, write, draw, paint, dance or call upon any other tool at your disposal. Use these tools to explore who you are and where you are going. You don't need to know where you want to go or what you want the future to hold in order to start this book. We will figure all that out together in these pages. Your life is not a spectator sport. It is not a static thing that happens to you. You build your life by choice.

Your life is not a spectator sport.

YOUR LIFE IS ALWAYS CHANGING AND GROWING

Your life is organic, always changing and growing. Career, education, interpersonal relationships, causes important to your heart—what direction all these amazing things take is your responsibility. There comes a calming satisfaction in knowing once you take the reins: it is your choice.

Many people struggle to communicate with and respect people with whom they don't agree. If you look around, the world is on the edge of massive changes. Economic struggle, political strife, and global pandemics exist on a level most of us have never seen before. We have lost each other and struggle to communicate with both our head and our heart engaged.

REACH OUT AND TAKE THIS OPPORTUNITY

This incredible opportunity requires your beautiful spirit to become involved in the wider world. To do that fully, in these difficult times, you need to build a solid foundation for yourself, honor your beliefs, and find your purpose.

That foundation also includes finding your community and being strong in who you are, even when those around you are different. This book is filled with those building materials: fun and creative activities, prompts and questions to keep things moving along.

If that sounds daunting or confusing, don't worry. Turning the pages of this book, you will be creating and flying through your own unique star stream. With your knuckles tight at the helm of your own stellar sled, we will move through the universe together!

WHY DOES FIGURING ALL THIS OUT MATTER?

Why is all this self-searching so important?
Without understanding your own beliefs, values, goals, or what brings you joy, you make yourself a "blank slate," so to speak. Who do you want filling that blank slate? Yourself? Or someone else?

As you grow and age the people who raised you play less of an active role in shaping who you are. New people, be they bosses, spouses, partners, friends, family, teachers, or others, may step into that influential space. Choose those people with care.

Sometimes those relationships may be out of your control. As the old saying goes, you can't control other people, but you can control your response to them. You decide how people will impact you: you get to control to what degree you allow someone into your life; you dictate who or what shapes your choices, values, and all the things that make you, YOU!

THE IMPORTANCE OF DISCERNMENT

One of the most important things you can do to honor yourself is to be discerning and intentional when allowing people into your life. Being discerning in your life is to understand what is true or appropriate for you. It is being able to judge and discriminate between the traits, behaviors, and values of those around you and decide what works for you. You can do this by watching how people treat you and others. Give yourself time to observe and understand people's actions and behaviors as you start new relationships. Also, being aware of your own feelings as you interact with someone. Trusting yourself and honoring your feelings is important to following the path of discernment.

HOW DOES THIS BOOK HELP YOU?

This book will help you to discover, honor, and develop your dreams. It will also teach you the tools to love and care for yourself—because there is nobody on the planet like you. I hope this book helps you see yourself as the precious sparkle of universal stardust that you are.

There are so many pieces and parts to our lives. We might be a sister or a daughter, we might be a student or a worker, we might be bipolar, we might be very devout in our religious beliefs, we might be transitioning in our sexuality. These are all intersections of who we are. The term "intersectionality" was coined by Dr. Kimberlé Crenshaw, a law professor at Columbia and UCLA, and writer and teacher of feminist thought. This term is helpful to consider as you examine all of the parts and pieces of your life.

THE INTERSECTIONALITY OF YOUR LIFE

Intersectionality is the culmination of all our different pieces and parts and how they work together to make us a unique individual not duplicated anywhere in the universe. Our values, spiritual beliefs, background, mental health, political beliefs, heritage, sexuality, profession, and the many other ways we socially define ourselves, make us each a person unlike any other. We are not "just this" or "just that."

We are a collection of amazing things.

ALL YOUR PIECES AND PARTS ARE PRECIOUS

However, society may not always view our intersections as "amazing," and bringing that to light was the focus of Kimberlé Crenshaw's work. She is a teacher of feminist thought and writer on demarginalizing race and sex as a way of describing the overlap of social identities.

Our work here is to say YES! Every piece and part of you is worthy, precious, and honorable.

Even your shadow parts are precious. The parts you struggle with, reject, or push away, and may not be ready to take on are all worth cherishing and examining. They make you who you are. You are valuable, which means that they are valuable. That's something to stay focused on through our journey forward.

WHAT'S IN THE BOOK?

This book is not for the faint of heart.

The fact that you even picked this book up means you are one of the few young women who has the bravery to create a different kind of life for yourself. This book is for seekers, for warriors, for discoverers. The work you do in this book will test you, but I promise that it will be worth the effort . . .

This journey of self-discovery will be something you carry with you for the rest of your life. We will start by creating a "tool kit" and then off we will go, moving into the next parts of this amazing adventure together.

Mercy me!

Getting Ready

To prepare for the following chapters I suggest finding a favorite journal. If you don't have an awesome journal you haven't cracked open yet, maybe try to find one that feels really special. Do you have to drop a huge chunk of change? Nope! A writing tablet, a pile of computer paper, a composition notebook you haven't used will do just fine but make it special. Draw in it, include pictures, lyrics, bedazzle it, whatever makes it yours. Okay, let's get to it.

Chapter 2: Your Tool Kit

The tool kit we will create together in Chapter Two is going to help you build a foundation for your journey. This tool kit will be your own personal survival guide to support you going forward. The tool kit chapter is almost entirely about self-care. How do we do it? What is it? Why is it important? We'll explore how having an awareness of your overall wellness—body, mind, and spirit—helps create the life you want. The tool kit will help you build a physical, emotional, mental, and spiritual self-care routine that will grow and expand with you in all areas of your life.

Chapter 3: Self-Love

Next we come to Chapter Three: Self-Love. You will confront your values, self-image, and the persona everyone around you sees. What does that little voice in your heart and head whisper to you about yourself?

Know that you do not have to be perfect. NO ONE IS PERFECT! Honoring who YOU are, instead of constantly comparing yourself to others or berating your own abilities is a skill guaranteed to leave you feeling empowered!

Chapter Three will include exercises, resources, and activities to help you sift through these crucial parts of yourself.

Chapter 4: Journey to Connection

Relationships, as we all know, can be challenging. Certain relationships feel like you've wound up in the middle of a cactus patch instead of a tiptoe through the tulips. Cactus patches can be incredible teachers. Painful, difficult times feel like they will last forever, but THEY DO NOT. They too will pass, and as they do, they show us our own values. Picking a relationship's "cactus needles" out of your heels, elbows, and anywhere else they may have landed is fundamental to cultivating relationships that will allow you to grow and care for yourself and connect to others in your life.

In Chapter Four, we will be taking a hard look at the different relationships in your life. Understanding these relationships deepens opportunities for love, growth, and connection. You will investigate your past interactions with friends, significant others, siblings and yes . . . PARENTS. Yikes! Just like I said . . . we're going to be needing that tool kit!

Keeping people around you that are positive and supportive even though you may not always agree is an important key to nurturing your spark.

We struggle with friends, classmates, co-workers, mean girls, haters, and a gauntlet of other nasty characters. You get to decide who is on "Team Awesome," your team, the people you choose to have in your life. Don't ever forget that the spots on your team—your inner circle—are for those who can provide you with reciprocal trust, support, and love.

Chapter 5: Warrior Soul

Our next deep dive is Chapter Five: Warrior Soul. Living in our world can be challenging, even on a good day. This chapter is about finding your spiritual and physical heroes—those "warriors" who inspire you. These are people, living or dead, real or imagined, that you admire, not the day-to-day tribe of people around you.

These are the icons, archetypes, and heroes that you aspire to be like or take important lessons from. They are your protectors, guides, and models as you chase your own dreams.

This chapter works on using these warriors to protect your spark and treasuring those things you hold close through honoring them. Who are your heroes, guardians, spiritual protectors? How are you like them? How can you use the examples laid out by these guides to develop your warrior self? How can you protect what is sacred and make your dreams a reality? Nobody does it alone. Remember what you have learned from your warriors and be on the lookout for other warriors-in-training, like you. Seeing the warrior's soul in others will help ignite your own.

Chapter 6: North Star

Our final self-improvement chapter is "North Star." After we do all our work in the aforementioned chapters, we should be feeling connected to the world around us. Then it's time to step away from the human, material world and see the bigger picture.

The "North Star" chapter looks at your spiritual journey and your sacred connection to the world and the Earth. The stork didn't just drop you from the sky you know! From the day you were born you have been on a spiritual journey seeking a connection to your "Source." If you let yourself follow it, where will that journey take you? That's what we will look at in the "North Star" chapter.

Included in Each Chapter

At the end of chapters 3-6 you will find journaling prompts and creative activities. If you don't like journaling, try the creative activities; if you don't like those, use the bullet pointed "Things to Think About" at the start of each chapter. If that doesn't work, pull something out of the tool kit you will create. There is something for everybody no matter how you like to engage!

WHAT'S THE TAKEAWAY?

Sometimes our experiences feel like a thousand splendid suns' worth of joy: we get a promotion or get into a program we have worked hard for; we meet someone incredible; we convey the exact expression or emotion we imagined on the face of a figure we are painting. But other times it's a bad moon rising, filling us with dread. Someone we care for passes away, we lose a job, or get a rejection letter, or we really let somebody down. It's up to you to use the skills you'll learn in this book to find the joyous in the difficult and to make use of what you take away from these pages.

You can't stop the good and the bad of life from happening, but you can try to stay mindful and understand that life ebbs and flows. The horrible won't last forever and it's important to enjoy good things as they happen, but remember it's all part of the journey. We can't appreciate the light if we've never seen the dark. It's important to cherish the pain, losses, and mistakes as well as the accomplishments, gifts, and joys. As you live your life remain focused on your Foundation—your core relationships, values, and spiritual beliefs. Only then will you discover your path to be one of love and care for both yourself, and those you cherish. What is right? What is important? What are my dreams and how do I reach them? Keep reading to discover all those answers and more.

Geronimo!

WHAT DO I DO NOW?

Whew!! I know this feels like a lot! Rome wasn't built in a day, as they say. Go slow and steady. Take this book at the pace that is right for you. You may set aside 10 minutes a day to read and explore it bit by tiny bit, you may read this book in one sitting, engulfing yourself in words of self-discovery, love, and joy. You may read this book chapter by chapter, leaving time for thought and reflection as each concept is introduced and explored. Who knows, maybe it will be the book you take on your morning commute. The important part is to start! You may move quicker through some concepts and exercises than others but, no matter what, you GOT this! I'm so glad you made the choice to be here. I honor the love, light, truth, and peace within you for taking this time and starting this journey! The Universe within is waiting!

Ready? Get set . . . GO!

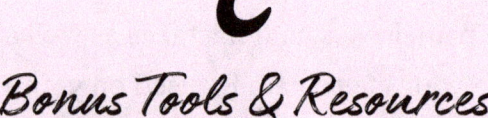

Bonus Tools & Resources

Follow along as I do the creative activities in each chapter, and get extra tips and resources including:

- ♥ A virtual meditation room
- ♥ Inspiring music playlists for Apple Music & Spotify
- ♥ Creative activities
- ♥ Extra ideas & topics
- ♥ And more!

Find it at: www.mysparkjourney.com

2
Your Tool Kit

Things to Think About

He who has health has hope. He who has hope has everything. —Arabian Proverb

Self-care is giving the world the best of you, instead of what's left of you. —Katie Reed

Take time today to love yourself. You deserve it. —Avina Celeste

BUILDING YOUR TOOL KIT

Hey everybody, get the Starbucks, the LIFEWTR, light some incense—whatever is needed to sit yourself down and get comfortable. You've got an amazing tool kit to assemble! Why do you need a tool kit? A tool kit is a group of strategies that you design, proven to work for you, which filters out negative forces and lets you navigate life with: less fear, more happiness and more personal fulfillment. Taking ownership and diving into your tool kit teaches you what your specific needs are, what life patterns work best for you, and what your joys are.

WHAT'S IN THE TOOL KIT?

Your expanding tool kit will help you complete some of the exercises in this book and grow in a variety of unexpected, positive ways. The tool kit includes self-care work, goal work, healing work, self-esteem work, and finding and accepting who you truly are. Your tool kit can be a powerful resource to turn to throughout your life, if you so choose.

WAYS TO USE YOUR TOOL KIT

So first, let me explain the layout of the kit. This chapter will give you space to dream, research, make changes, grow, scribble, take notes, add things in, cross things out—whatever you want! You can use the tool kit if you are having a stressful day at work, or school, or you may be in a place in life where you are making difficult decisions. The tool kit is there to support you. If you receive a personal revelation while driving or watching a movie, or whatever the case may be, you can continue to add new ideas to your kit.

My wish is that wherever you go, whatever you may be doing, you use your tool kit to continue your journey of self-care and discovery. In addition to adding all the strategies and ideas for self-care you come up with, you can also start adding favorite quotes, song lyrics, memories or pictures of loved ones, drawings, stickers, anything that makes it your own. Your tool kit should be a happy, feel-good place.

HOW TO START BUILDING YOUR TOOL KIT

This chapter will ask questions, make suggestions, and start you thinking about and researching places, things, people, and activities of your choosing. These are things that calm you, provide a healthy mental attitude and bring you joy. The chapter is

Tool Kit Support System

Your tool kit support system also has a support system! On SPARK! Soul Therapy, on YouTube, you will find a video on building and "blinging" your tool kit. Plus, on my website www.mysparkjourney.com, you'll find a separate, downloadable version for purchase that has loads of extra writing and "blinging" space so you don't have to lug your entire journal around.

broken into sections of wellness, and you come up with what works for you. Some of the areas are physical, social, spiritual etc. You can start scribbling notes and ideas here. You can include places you want to contact for more information, things you want to research on your phone, etc. The tool kit is about collecting things that provide you with wellness and stability and having them all in one place that is easy to access, beautiful, blingy, and creative.

YOU JUST NEED TO START

These pages don't need to be perfect—you just need to start! Start coming up with ideas and activities that will work for YOU. As things occur to you, scribble them down and add them later. No rules. Only freedom. You decide.

YOUR TOOL KIT GROWS AND CHANGES WITH YOU

Your tool kit is an organic entity, changing and growing along with you. Feeling safe, healthy, and cared for should change as you mature emotionally.

WHEN TO USE YOUR TOOL KIT

When should we grab our portable support system? It could be a fight with a friend or a parent, failing a test, losing a job, moving, being granted a scholarship, accepting a new job, a marriage proposal, working way too many shifts in a row, getting first chair in the jazz band—all things "good crazy" and "bad crazy," can throw us off our mark. It is times like those where your tool kit will help you to take time and catch your breath, to breathe. Honor that need.

HONOR THE GOOD CRAZY AND THE BAD CRAZY

More difficult circumstances will come. It could be a difficult or severe medical diagnosis, the loss of a loved one, or any other personal tragedy. Life, at times, can feel more like a struggle than anything else; if you've been alive long enough, you know exactly what I'm talking about! Those things will always happen to us in our lives.

The important part is creating support and awareness within and without your being.

This will allow you to move through life from a place of steadfastness and balance instead of clinging to the swinging pendulum wondering what's coming next.

PREPARATION IS THE KEY

You need to prepare yourself for self-care, so that when you need it all of your strategies are safely stowed away in your tool kit. This preparation can build a solid foundation for yourself, your beliefs, your purpose in life, and caring for yourself. Having a solid foundation allows you to know how to care for yourself and remain steady through the ups and downs as they present themselves.

THE GOOD AND THE BAD DON'T LAST

Your tool kit should remind you that no one state of being or feeling lasts forever. This too will end and something new will begin. Such is the impermanent nature of life.

DISCERNMENT

The more you know about what you are feeling and who you are, the more discerning you become. I mentioned discernment very briefly in Chapter One. Discernment means the ability to assess or to judge.

The more you understand yourself the more you can discern what is right for you.

As I said earlier, it is being able to judge and discriminate between the traits, behaviors, and values of those around you and decide what works for you. You can do this by watching how people treat you and others.

HOW DO YOU DISCERN?

Give yourself time to observe and understand people's actions and behaviors as you start new relationships. You learn to start looking through the lens of who you are and making decisions in your life through that lens. There is so much noise in the world: social media, 600 TV channels, a zillion online podcasts, blogs, and streams. There is so much coming at you. Your ability to discern in this world, through your own personal lens, is absolutely crucial to a balanced, healthy life.

START WITH SELF CHECK-INS

How do you know what you need and when you need it? Start by practicing self check-ins. Tune into how you are feeling at various times throughout your day. Stop and ask yourself: what exactly am I feeling at this moment? Am I angry, happy, sad, lonely, confused, remorseful, elated, grieving or any of the hundreds of other feelings on the human emotional spectrum? What can you do to either nurture or move through that emotion? It can be difficult if you don't have prior experience. You CAN do it. It just takes time and practice.

LOOKING AT YOUR FEELINGS

When you stop and ask all those questions you have to be ready for the answer. There may be physical responses, emotional responses, thoughts, or memories that help you to understand what you are feeling. That's OK.

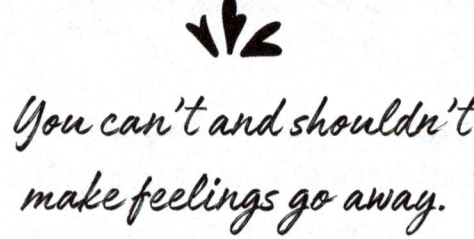

You can't and shouldn't make feelings go away.

Experience your feelings, know they are there for a reason. Pick strategies from your tool kit that will keep you centered and identify the things you need in that moment. That's why frequent self check-ins can be so vital. Only by staying aware of our feelings can we truly understand them. If you start to feel really overwhelmed at certain points it's okay to slow down, save certain memories or parts of your life until you feel ready for them, talk to a therapist, whatever you need, do it.

NOW WE START BUILDING!

Below are some tips you can use to build your tool kit. I suggest circling the things you know work for you and write in any missing parts. Spend some time here! This is one of the most important parts of this journey and helps to create a life that brings you joy and a truly conscious existence.

THE TOOL KIT IS YOURS: ADD, EXPAND, ENUMERATE

As I mentioned before, you can build on this tool kit and use it for the rest of your life. If there are categories missing or things that need adding, take the time now and do that. Look at each section, decide what additional things you would add to the categories based on things you love and enjoy. Building on and using your tool kit can help put you on a pathway to self-discovery and steady footing.

FIGURING OUT WHAT YOU NEED

It's important to recognize that your body and soul may need different things at different times. Honor how your body responds. That's why I created different categories to prepare you for different needs and circumstances. As you build your kit you continue to learn what works for you and what doesn't. The kit helps you build a physical, emotional, mental, and spiritual self-care routine that will grow and expand over time. You can use it in all areas of your life.

GETTING STARTED

1. Find and create a pool of activities for your lists. Creating a wide range of options helps you navigate all kinds of circumstances. Select the tool that works for you at that moment.

2. Pick tools for a variety of time frames. Some activities may take you only half a minute to complete. Others may take minutes or even hours of reflection and thought. The goal is to find what works and makes sense for you. Come up with exercises that can help you both long-term and short-term.

3. Certain tools may go in more than one category. Put them in one, put them in both . . . it's up to you.

4. Your tool kit is magically, specifically, and creatively yours.

5. Your tool kit can be your own private lifeline to positivity, joy and self-care.

6. Create your tool kit in your own time frame.

7. For example, if you find yourself in the midst of a panic attack, it is often difficult to reach for a selection of tools to calm down. Make sure you put some very simple ideas in your kit such as breathing techniques, or a list of favorite, calming places you can visualize easily.

8. I once met a woman who, when stuck in a classroom with limited options, used to count ceiling tiles when she felt a panic attack coming on. For each tile she counted, she took a breath. I want you to think of things like that—that only last seconds and can get you out of a tough mental situation. If that is something you face, use this type of solution as an example.

9. To some people having a free Saturday would feel like heaven on earth. To others, a day with no structure may cause them panic, depression and feelings of worthlessness or restlessness. Use your tool kit and ask yourself these questions: Am I feeling lonely, or just alone? What's the difference? What activities make me happy, or at least distract me from racing thoughts? How do I treat myself when I am alone? While it is okay to give people their space, when was the last time I reached out to friends and family? What am I curious about? Passionate about? What scares me? What have I always wanted to try doing? What would I do right now if I asked myself to make a spontaneous decision? It doesn't matter what it might be—a walk, a trip to your favorite coffee shop, painting, dancing, and anything else that helps you recharge and refresh!

SEEK, INVESTIGATE, CHALLENGE, EXPLORE

Preparing this tool kit is a great opportunity to test, seek out, and investigate new and novel things in your life. New experiences are perfect for filling your kit. What's a goal you're working towards? A new challenge you've set for yourself? A new adventure you've yet to go on—all of these build up your life and sustain you. They make you feel accomplished, rested, satisfied and calm.

UPDATE AS YOU CHANGE

As you go through life, your tool kit will grow and change with you. Your kit will expand as you get better at honoring your own likes and dislikes. Life is not a static thing. Your life is organic and always changing. Much in the same way, your tool kit should be a living, evolving entity. Like life, it grows and moves through orbits and phases in the most conscious, joyful way possible, if you let it.

START BUILDING YOUR TOOL KIT!

The following sections are different categories of tools for you to put into your tool kit. Within each topic, there are a number of ways to get yourself started and commonly used techniques I will share.

Relax Your Mind

These are the things we do when we need to rest and unplug from the world around us. Consider the techniques in this category when you really need a break.

Some things here might include:

- Deep breathing
- Progressive relaxation
- Naps
- Meditation
- The Insight Timer app provides varying lengths of relaxing music and videos
- Try a guided meditation in the HeadSpace app, or another service of your choosing
- Find your local holistic shop and see if they offer Gong baths, or other forms of sound therapy
- Pray the rosary or meditate with a mala

It's wise to have some activities you can use even in the middle of the night, if you wake up, thoughts racing, and you have only your phone or mind as a means to calm yourself down. You can also add activities in the "Relax Your Mind" section that are a little more involved. Maybe you sign up for a meditation class once a week for a few months. Or maybe you go to a weekend prayer retreat. You can also create a relaxation schedule for yourself. Schedule deep breathing, guided meditation, walks, cooking lessons—anything that helps you center and relax your mind.

Scheduled Practice Builds Routine

By making those exercises part of your daily scheduled routines, you're more likely to follow through on them, gain increased confidence and gain fluency with your tool kit. There are endless options for self-care with your tool kit. Be ready (and open) for anything. Take some time and pursue what you are interested in. Ask yourself: what makes you feel calm, safe, and centered? List the things that you know work for you, and things you want to try going forward. As I have said, this will be an evolving and changing list as the years go by.

Relax Your Body

These following ideas can help release you from physical symptoms of anxiety, depression, helplessness or plain annoyance. This can either be achieved by calming your body down physically or burning off excess energy so that your body can bring itself back to baseline.

Sometimes It Helps to Get Moving

Though it may seem counterintuitive, sometimes dancing, running, working out, shooting hoops, swimming, walking or any physical activity can help. Tiring ourselves out, giving your body an influx of oxygen and focusing on a physical task can help your body settle itself down.

It's important to know when you need to physically blow off some steam and make sure you DO IT! Trying to sit calmly, or take deep breaths, when you are ready to hang from the ceiling by your fingernails is not going to be effective. Prepare the right tool for the right circumstance.

Deciding What Works Means Listening to Your Body

One of the most important things to remember is this: listen to your body.

Know when you are angry or frustrated and need to burn energy. Alternatively, know when you are sad, anxious, or feeling overwhelmed, you may need to do something else to feel calm and balanced. Only by learning and honoring your body's needs can you select the right technique from your tool kit when it comes time to calm down. It takes practice, but you are awesome—and you will get it, I just know it!

Some things here might include:

- ✻ Taking deep breaths
- ✻ Recite a mantra
- ✻ Use a guided meditation
- ✻ Go for a walk or run
- ✻ Do a body scan and breathe through stress points
- ✻ Shoot hoops
- ✻ Dance it out!

What are the things in this category that work for you? Add a few things you want to try for the future.

Relax Your Brain

I know I said "relax your mind" earlier. This is a little different. Our brains need rest too. Taking a break from life, while still being mentally active, can help keep you focused on a project, give yourself a "happy break" by doing a mental activity you love, and keep your mind sharp. These are tools to keep in mind when you want to get nagging or intrusive thoughts out of your brain.

Some Things Might Include:

* Reading books in your favorite genre or by a favorite author
* Sudoku, or other puzzles
* Podcasts on anything under the sun: history, how to grow an orchid, spooky stories, aliens—anything you can think of—there is a podcast for it! Sometimes just listening to someone else's voice telling you a story, or some useful or fun information, can really change your latitude and perspective. List them in this section then load them somewhere and have them ready to go.
* Music is a great relaxer (listening or playing) but be sure not to fall into an abyss of breakup songs or other negative situations. The music you choose for this purpose should have uplifting lyrics or be entirely instrumental. Remember, the goal is to help relax your brain—not overstimulate it with too many words or ideas.
* Knitting, or other thread and fabric activities can be a blast. So too can other forms of arts and crafts—find some that work for you.
* Gaming can be another way to engage your brain and calm down. If your goal is to relax, avoiding negative content like violence and warfare is a must. This type of relaxation should be

all gumdrops and lollipops.

- ✳ Watching a favorite old sitcom or cartoon can help cheer you up.
- ✳ YouTube videos exist on just about any topic in the world that may interest you. Art, photography, how to ride a horse—whatever appeals to you, there's likely a calming, informative video about it available online.
- ✳ Start a YouTube channel yourself and teach people something you are passionate about.

Add things that you know work for you and a few things you want to try for the future. List as many things as truly bring you joy or are worth investigating. You can change these lists as often as you like. New things constantly come to you as you live one day to the next.

Relax with Humor

This can be one of the greatest sections in your tool kit—make sure it's fully stocked! Humor can carry you through just about anything. It is sooooo essential to be able to laugh. Being silly and joyful in life is essential. The kind of laughter that makes you crack up, makes your belly ache and tears slip out the corner of your eyes is key for a well-adjusted life. What are things that really make you laugh? Make sure you identify them and have a place to experience those things when you need to laugh a little.

Things that belong in this category might be:

- ✳ Silly movies
- ✳ Sitcoms or YouTube silliness
- ✳ Jokes
- ✳ Memes

- Pinterest posts
- Silly dog or other animal antics

Whatever it is for you, make sure you identify it and tuck it away somewhere you can access it when you need it. Call a friend that has you cackling with laughter when you talk to them. Like the other parts of our tool kit, when it comes to humor, you should think of go-to things that can make you smile or laugh in a second or two, as well as humorous strategies for taking on the day, week, month or years! Always be building your humor file! Humor can carry the weight of tragedy, if used in the right way.

Social Relaxation

Sometimes when we get sad or anxious, we may isolate ourselves when we need to do the opposite. Some of us are just not that comfortable around people, which is okay. However, there are times when engaging with fellow human beings can be centering, refreshing and uplifting.

Sometimes socializing can feel like the most enjoyable thing ever and we don't have to push ourselves to engage. Other times we may need to be reminded how important it is to take time to be with the people we love, adore or just make us laugh. Especially as you get older, it may feel like you have fewer friends than you did when you were younger. Also, it can be harder to make new friends as we get older.

Always Be on the Lookout for New Friends

The truth is, you should always be on the lookout for new friends. Pay attention to the people around you. Look for shared values, and shared interests. We will explore what to look for in friendships and create a "deal breaker" list when it comes to relationships in the chapter, "Journey to Connection."

Don't put too much pressure on yourself. Your friends don't all have to be forever besties. Some people are just fun acquaintances with shared interests. Even if picking up the phone and calling somebody you don't talk to often feels challenging, it's important to stay connected. You will likely feel better having made that phone call than not.

If You're Uncomfortable . . . Practice

While it may sound a bit silly, you should practice having conversations with people. It can be almost anyone—chat up the checkout person at Target, talk to a coworker during your lunch break, or get to know a neighbor you haven't talked to much. If it's uncomfortable, start slow. You can do it. Just take it one step at a time. Do what you feel comfortable with, but don't forget that spending time with others is important. Even sitting in silence, being comfortably present with someone, is a true gift.

Some things that belong in this category might be:

- Time with friends
- A pleasant conversation
- Laughing with a friend
- Online gaming with people you know
- Going to the movies
- Lunch with an old acquaintance
- Taking a walk with someone
- A FaceTime call with a family member
- Sitting, enjoying Starbucks with just one friend
- Whatever social situations you are most comfortable with. It doesn't have to be a party to be beneficial—this is about doing what makes you happy with the people who make you happy.

Relaxing and Doing Good—Civic Engagement

Another important tool that helps us care for ourselves is caring for others. This category covers civic engagement and social activism. Because they have many similarities and overlap, I am joining the two. This should be work that you are passionate about, causes that you feel connected to or that are truly the work of your heart. While we could go into the weeds about the finer points of civic engagement and social activism, we'll focus on building our tool kit and leave sociological ponderings to doctoral theses.

What's the Difference between the Two?

In the United States, most high schools require graduates to accumulate "community service hours" to satisfy the graduation requirements. While some students jump into their volunteer experiences with gusto, for most teenagers this is a chore. What we are doing here is not a chore. It's about acting on what is important to you. I am explaining civic engagement as activities or involvement that is considerate or beneficial to the community around you. Activism is focusing on a particular cause to make change in the world around you. A sense of connection to a group or community, shared purpose and understanding heals us, the people around us, and the planet as a whole. There are countless ways to be involved.

Things That Belong in This Category Might Be:

* Food drives
* Volunteering for animal shelters
* Running a 5k for cancer
* Doing a community book drive so kids in domestic violence shelters have something positive to look at to help them feel calm.

- ✱ If you play an instrument, go and play it for an animal shelter where the animals are alone and scared.
- ✱ Start a drive at your local VFW to collect items for troops overseas.
- ✱ Write a letter for a local or school paper and share your view on something near to your heart.
- ✱ Write to your Representatives and Senators. You can google the format and the proper way to email a legislator if you haven't done it before. Mostly, be clear, be concise and be respectful.
- ✱ Sell some sketches or artwork you made to raise money for a local food pantry or to help a neighbor from losing their home.

However you want to be involved, just do it! The list of things you can do to lift up the world around you is endless!

Guess what!?

Your tool kit is complete!

You did it!!! You made your kit! Nice Job!!! Well done, beautiful you!!!

Put on your favorite jam and take a 20-second dance break!

TOOL KIT WRAP UP

Every being on this planet has purpose. Every time we interact with a person, an animal, or thing, we continue to fulfill a part of our purpose. Make sure to treat yourself with love and kindness. Throughout our whole lives we wonder about our purpose on this planet. Many times throughout your journey you may be unsure of your purpose, but it's important to learn grounding and self-care techniques to keep moving forward.

The more we can prepare and do that in a crazy, fun, joyful, creative way, the easier it gets! Tough times will always come and go, but if we hang on to what helps us get through them, we can hold on until things shift back in our favor. It will shift. It will change. That's where the saying "This too shall pass" came from.

In the meantime . . .

Woo Hoo!! . . .

Well done . . .

On we go!!! . . .

Tool Kit Download

There is a separate downloadable version of the tool kit for purchase on www.mysparkjourney.com

3
Self-Love

Things to Think About

Love and care for yourself just as you are.

To love oneself is the beginning of a lifelong romance. —Oscar Wilde

I now see how owning our story and loving ourselves through the process is the bravest thing we will ever do. —Brené Brown

EVERYTHING BEGINS AND ENDS WITH LOVE

Hey! Welcome to the "Self-Love" chapter! The awesome tool kit we just created will help while working in this chapter. One of the most crucial things we can do in our lifetime is learn to love ourselves. It's life-long work. Self-love is a state of appreciating yourself with thoughts and actions that support your physical, psychological, and spiritual growth and health. It takes continuous practice because we are organic, dynamic beings and it's an ongoing process to support ourselves in a healthy, positive way.

One of the most crucial things we can do in our lifetime is learn to love ourselves.

When we support ourselves in this way it helps us to remain stable and connected during the highs and lows of life. Instead of gripping tightly to the pendulum as it swings back and forth from joy to crisis we learn to remain in balance and are able to watch the pendulum with some distance knowing that things change and struggles and joys of the moment won't last forever. If we continue to do our work what will last is our grounded, calm center that is able to manage the ebb and flow of life. Loving ourselves improves our emotional resilience, helps build solid self-image and self-esteem and can help keep anxiety and depression at bay. It is not easy to manage all the negatives in our lives. Especially the ones we foster because they have been with us as "close friends" or "familiars" for much of our lives.

Instead of living in the chaos these patterns can bring I propose we take another path. **I propose we take a path of self-acceptance, self-care, and self-love that allows us to reach for the stars.** Learn to let go of these little demons inside and work towards a higher existence. Work towards something that allows your spirit and dreams to move beyond and soar amongst the cosmos.

Once you have gotten a handle on the nasties that we will address in this chapter you will have the opportunity to start a new narrative in your life.

I propose we take a path of self-acceptance, self-care, and self-love that allows us to reach for the stars.

FIND YOUR TRUE SELF

That narrative is a true picture of your unique self. Moving towards understanding what you see within yourself. You can choose to see the negative in things and bring yourself down, or you can create something more positive and see the present and the future with positivity, curiosity, and expanded thinking. Both of these realities can be true. In your life you can choose the one that helps you feel uplifted and content. Create a thought pattern and a life tapestry that's higher, richer, and more fulfilling. Replace negative patterns with things that are honoring and uplifting and move you forward in a healthy, positive way. It's a day-to-day growth process that can change our trajectory in life. It's important work.

HOW DOES SELF-LOVE HELP

Self-love helps you feel safer and confident and reminds you nobody is perfect, and you certainly don't need to be. It helps us to learn when expectations might be unrealistic. It helps us be more mindful and present. Self-love helps us understand how to live in a place of gratitude and self-care. You can't love yourself without understanding and accepting yourself and your journey. I remember listening to an interview with former first lady Michelle Obama. Mrs. Obama expressed she had the most amazing, supportive husband in the world: "I am living with a man who loves me dearly, who thinks that the sun rises, and sets (by me) and he is clear and vocal about that and I get that affirmation every day, but I have to be honest sometimes that isn't enough because in the end the messages have to come from me. I have to believe it. I have to love myself. That's the work I have to do inside." That's the work all of us have to do inside and it's lifelong work.

LEARNING TO LOVE OURSELVES

How do we learn to love ourselves? There are a lot of answers to that question but one of the ways we can start is by listening to ourselves. We need to hear how we talk to ourselves and how we treat ourselves. We need to examine our thoughts, our behaviors, our feelings and start to weed out unhealthy patterns, and the negative pieces of ourselves that get stuck and cause us shame and guilt. Those can cause us to not love ourselves even though others may love us and see our beauty. This chapter shows you how to see our own beauty, take a look at what's going on inside and outside of yourself, and how you perceive it all in your life.

HOW DO WE PRACTICE SELF-LOVE?

Some of the ways you can practice self-love and learn a self-love routine are tackling negative self thinking and learning to set boundaries with yourself and others. Additionally, having emotional check-ins, honoring and validating yourself, and having people in your life that support and honor you are also invaluable tools.

Self-forgiveness for past mistakes is another self-love practice. Living in a mindset of gratitude and noticing and letting go of self-doubt is yet another. Love and accept your body in all the ways that beautiful machine takes care of you and allows you to live your life and accomplish things.

Also, staying joyful and curious in your life is an incredible way to love yourself. Honoring yourself, your being, your dignity is not always an easy thing. I'm going to take a moment here and talk about one of the more difficult ways we sabotage ourselves and dull our spark.

Weeding out unhealthy patterns in your life helps you unearth your true inner beauty.

LEARNING TO DEAL WITH NEGATIVE SELF-TALK

What is negative self-talk? Negative self-talk is having thoughts in your head that are really mean towards yourself. You call yourself names, stupid, ugly, or whatever your particular horrible inner voice tells you when you feel you have made a mistake, such as, feeling as if you thought something wrong, did something wrong, felt something wrong. We can be relentless in finding ways to internally beat up on ourselves. We all have that little band of bandits, (come up with your own visual) with sticks and clubs, living in our head.

They yell things that aren't very nice and shake their clubs and rail against you trying to break you down telling you how messed up you are, or how you shouldn't do that, think that, say that, you are so stupid because you got that question wrong, you're ugly, untalented, unlovable.

Those criminals can take up a lot of headspace if you let them. What do you do with this negative talk? We've all heard the story of people that are scared to give a speech and they imagine their audience in their underwear to avoid the fear and negative perceptions we put in our own heads. It helps if you can find a way to shrink that little "bandit boat" that's railing in your head down to Lego size and send it on its way.

FIRST YOU NEED TO HEAR YOUR NEGATIVE SELF-TALK

The first thing I want you to do with negative self-talk is to hear it clearly. Notice where and when it pops up and exactly what the most popular terms you hear are. Don't let it continue to slip by with a 1-2 punch and keep moving on its way. As I said about your tool kit, I want you to spend some time here. How you think about yourself and how much time you spend treating yourself negatively is a very important piece to get a hold of. I can tell you from working for years with women, young and old, that we women are SO hard on ourselves in the area of negative-self talk, myself included! Everything from calling yourself stupid, ugly, lazy, and the like, to telling yourself all of the things you will never accomplish or how dare you think you could do that.

ONCE YOU HEAR IT, NEUTRALIZE IT

It's important to pull these thoughts out and let them know you know they are there and they will not be tolerated any longer. Identify them clearly. Write down what the most common painful words or phrases are that you tell yourself. Notice it throughout your day and jot those little scoundrels down. Understand that they are not true. They are usually exaggerations, or extortions that our consciousness drags out when we are anxious, unsure, or afraid. Because they are nothing more than stress noises; those words don't make you who you are or become true unless you let them.

Still, it can be tricky to get a handle on negative talk. Sometimes you continue to build it up, continually repeat it to yourself. You worry about it ahead of time and for a long time after a situation has ended. There is a saying that says, "there are two things you shouldn't worry about: the things you can change and the things you can't change." If you can change it, great! Get to it. If you can't change it, don't worry about it, just keep moving forward and focus on the positives and the "can do's." Being consumed with negative thoughts, complaining, and beating up on yourself leaves you stuck and beat down instead of invigorated and hopeful, which is what allows you to make positive changes in your life.

SHUTTING IT DOWN TAKES TIME AND PRACTICE

If negative self-talk is something you have been doing to yourself for years, it can be a hard thing to notice and bring into the bright light. Remind yourself it is just brain noise and old patterns. It sounds difficult but, with patience and perseverance, dispelling the negative can be done. And it's important that you do it. It's important to take out the stinky garbage in your brain that doesn't serve you or help you on your journey.

We all beat ourselves up from time to time. From my clinical experience working with so many women, particularly when we are younger, we are wicked with how often we beat ourselves up with that brain noise. To some degree, society plays a definite role in this, but that talk is for another day. It can be so harmful to your being to continually berate, belittle and beat up yourself from the inside out.

Jalima's Story

Jalima was terrified of going to high school every day. She would sometimes have panic attacks at night if it was going to be a particularly difficult day the next day. She had a huge arsenal of negative thoughts that would run through her day as she went class to class and interacted with the people around her. Slowly, she started replacing some of that thinking. When she started thinking about all the things that could go wrong throughout the day, she started to replace those individual thoughts and circumstances with what could go right. Things she was excited about, "I'm looking forward to seeing so and so," "I am doing great in this particular class," or "I really am looking forward to seeing a particular teacher today."

When Jalima would say to herself, "I feel anxious," she would start to think, "I feel excited. I have an excited energy in me that I can use how I like. I'm feeling excitement inside myself." That takes out the fear of the situation and replaces it with a different perception. Getting out of negative thoughts is about changing your perception and changing your focus of what's around you. I'm not saying it's easy; I'm saying with practice, patience, and perseverance it can be done. In picking up this book you've made the decision to try.

Steps to Freeing Yourself of Negative Thoughts

If you want to start getting free of negative self-talk, try these steps:

- ♥ Start identifying the negative words or phrases and write them down.

- ♥ Make a statement to those words or thoughts that they need to hit the road, however that sounds to you.

- ♥ Build a new, more realistic thought pattern. Show those exaggerations for what they are. You are not a failure because you did poorly on one test or project, etc.. These are normal parts of life.

- ♥ Put some new thoughts into the mix. Remind yourself of some positives. Things you are good at. Things you have done you were proud of.

BOUNDARIES ARE SELF-LOVE

Not all of our struggles are on the inside. Sometimes people invade your person in ways you don't expect. They may try to push their beliefs on you or make you feel invalidated for believing what you believe or being who you are. This is the time when we need to be aware of and set our personal boundaries.

WHAT IS A BOUNDARY?

What exactly is a boundary? In terms of relationships with other humans, it is the line where your being ends and another person begins. More clearly, where your values, identity, responsibility, sense of control and autonomy exist and where someone else's concept of those things commingle. Does it sound difficult? It can be tricky which is why I'm adding it to this book. It can be much less difficult if you know who you are, what you value, and what's a negotiation or a deal breaker in relationship interactions. Yes, it's complicated. Yes, we don't always have all the information, or make the best choices. That's okay! It's about learning. Learning to say no, learning to accept ourselves and stand our ground, and in our power, and learning to appreciate that our voice matters.

All boundaries have a psychological element to how they affect us. When we come away from an interaction with someone feeling shamed, belittled, angry or sad it could just be that we have disagreed or are having a momentary struggle with that person. On the other hand, if it's something that continues to happen with that person on a variety of issues, or on the same issue with various people, we may need to check in and see if we have set proper boundaries for ourselves.

TYPES OF BOUNDARIES

Emotional Boundaries

Boundaries around feelings and emotions are very common boundaries that need to be set. Learning what you are comfortable sharing with others, and who you feel safe with emotionally, is an important boundary to set. Sharing your deepest, darkest secrets with someone you don't trust, haven't known for long, or who posts everything on social media, may not be the best person to share with. It may leave you feeling violated or dishonored.

Examples of What These Situations Look Like and What to Do

If someone is constantly critical when you express your feelings or won't honor your feelings and needs when you express them, it might be time to set some boundaries and address the issue. We all have times when we need different things but when someone chronically dismisses you it's time to look at the issue. Once you start setting boundaries out of the gate in relationships, things will look and feel very different.

Examples of ways you can express your boundaries:

1. I feel invalidated when you criticize me in that way (be specific).
2. I feel hurt when you don't consider my point of view.
3. I feel attacked when you make statements like that (be specific).
4. I feel really disrespected when you respond like that (be specific).

Physical Boundaries

Physical boundaries are related to your physical comfort level and physical safety.

You have the right to feel comfortable in any situation without feeling pressured or obligated by anybody. Physical boundary violations can have to do with someone who doesn't respect your personal space. In a more benign sense, someone who is a "close talker," in a not so benign sense, it is someone who stands close or invades your space to try to intimidate you or control a situation. Stepping away from a situation and taking a timeout is always an acceptable option. Be aware when you need to do that and do it.

More Physical Boundaries and What to Do

Another part of physical boundaries and how someone might violate them is unwanted touch, public displays of affection that are uncomfortable, unwanted sexual advances, harassment through touch, or sexual assault from a stranger, dating partner, relationship partner or marriage partner. All these relationships can have boundary violations. I know that this is really heavy stuff, but the sooner you can identify the signs the better your chances are for setting the boundaries you want and need and taking care of yourself in the best ways you can.

Examples of ways you can express your boundaries:

1. I am not comfortable when you touch me like that. I need you to stop that.

2. I am not comfortable doing that in public

3. I need you to step back a foot . . . or two or three . . . it's your comfort level.

Financial Boundaries

Another area you can struggle with related to boundaries are financial boundaries. These boundaries have to do with how you see money and how you share and interact around money. Many marriages and relationships break up over arguments around money. It's important to know what you think about money. Are you a saver? Do you spend every last penny the second you get some money? Do you have certain things you love that you spend tons of money on and in other areas of your life you are very tight with spending?

When you interact with people around money it can be difficult. Do you go to lunch with coworkers and there is always that one person who won't pay their share when the check comes? Do you have friends, family or a relationship partner always asking to borrow money and they don't pay it back? Do you have someone always expecting you to pay when you go out with them or weaseling away when the bill comes? Have you struggled with shared mortgages, apartments, or other living arrangements where you feel things aren't fair or you are being taken advantage of? These are all issues around financial boundaries.

It's important to know if you are a saver or a spender and under what circumstances. It's important to share with people what your comfort level is in spending situations ahead of time. It's OK to ask! I know it feels uncomfortable but it's important.

Examples of ways you can express your boundaries:

1. How are we going to divide this up before we start?
2. My budget doesn't allow that this week but maybe next week?
3. I'm saving for a Caribbean cruise so I can't do that with you right now.
4. No, I can't help you right now. (You don't have to apologize.)

ARE YOU BOUNDARY CROSSING?

We also need to look at the possibility that we may be invading other people's boundaries and not realizing it. The best way to set and hold boundaries is clear, respectful communication about what your wants, needs, and expectations are in the relationship or circumstance.

Other people have their own boundaries and we need to be aware that things might not always match up and so another piece to boundaries is understanding and respecting other peoples. What types of boundaries are there in your relationships and what do we prepare for?

STANDING UP FOR YOURSELF

Boundaries can be really hard at times and feel really good when you hold them in place. Setting boundaries can eliminate the extra stress, guilt, shame, or discomfort that not speaking up for yourself can cause. It's always important to set your boundaries and express yourself with "I" statements. I feel, I want, etc. What the other person might feel or say is their business. It is not up to us to assume or blame them for their behavior. You are just stating what you feel and need from your perspective. Don't forget you are valid, you are precious, you are important, so speak up for yourself!

Setting proper boundaries in your life can help you skip one-hundred miles of bad road you didn't need to travel.

WATCH THINGS CHANGE

Lastly, if you need extra help with boundaries or situations that are really extreme, seek out a mental health professional or therapist. Many of these circumstances can be really tough or even dangerous and if we were raised with a lack of boundaries and have never put them in place, you may need some help. That's okay! That's awesome to do for yourself. Good for you!

The important part of setting boundaries is learning to look at how people treat you through the new lens of what makes you feel comfortable and respected as a human being. Based on what you see you can decide what to do next. Maybe you talk it through and you get to watch with excitement as things get better and you are not stressed, angry, or uncomfortable. Maybe if the person cannot honor you in any way that feels good to you, and nothing changes, you may decide to walk away and work on building relationships with people that you feel respect and care for you. It's hard work but you can absolutely build relationships worth having around your boundaries. You are worth it.

SELF-ACCEPTANCE = SELF-LOVE

Think about this, you are the only person on this planet that sees what you see in the way you see it. Think about how incredible that is. Playing small instead of honoring your incredible uniqueness doesn't serve anybody. Writer and activist Marianne Williamson wrote a poem called "Our Deepest Fear." Marianne says,"our deepest fear is not that we are inadequate but that we are powerful beyond measure," and basically, we think, how dare we. It scares the hell out of us to let our individual light flood the world, ignite our spark, and let the world see. But I say that's exactly what we need to do!

BE WHO YOU ARE BECAUSE YOU'RE AWESOME

You need to be who, and what, you are in the strongest way possible. If that strength is being soft-spoken, kind and passionate, or loud as a lion it matters that you express it. We need to be able to engage our dreams and passions, honor our strengths and help others to do the same. When you accept yourself, and you engage in relationships with others, you do it from a place of validation and love for yourself and the other person, whether you agree with their vision of life or not. You can listen, try to understand, and still respect your own feelings and values. Deep listening and treating others with dignity and honoring our own dignity fuels our hearts and supports our independence and self-reliance. It's important to find your way, your voice, and the self-love to honor who you are meant to be.

WHAT WE VALUE

I wrote this chapter so you can do work on what is inside of you. Self-acceptance and self-love are the biggest pieces of that. What values do you choose to portray to support that self-acceptance and self-love? What does your core look like? How do you see yourself? How do you show yourself love? What do you want to show the world? It's time to take a look at yourself and what you value.

What are the benefits of looking at who you are on the inside? Understanding how you see yourself and the value of loving what you see, lets your thoughts, actions, and expressions have purpose in your life. Knowing, and standing by what you value, helps you honor and love who you are as a human being. Honoring and feeling confident in who you are can ignite passion for your goals and dreams, provide a deep sense of strength in who you are and give you an inner contentment.

WHEN WE DON'T HONOR OURSELVES

When you don't follow and honor what you value, it can cause feelings of not living and telling your truth. You may feel lost, and it can also create a feeling of dis-ease we can't quite put our finger on. Not one of us is perfect. Sometimes we stand up and project what we value and sometimes that doesn't happen like we hope it would. Life is a very complex thing with lots of moving parts. That's true for everyone. It is, however, important to identify what and who you value and why you value them clearly so it can provide you with the strength to go forward and live the dreams and goals that you've chosen and hold your boundaries when you need to.

THE ONLY REAL MISTAKES ARE THE ONES WE DON'T LEARN FROM

We will all make mistakes and be someone we don't like at some time or another. So what! Be aware of your thoughts and actions, keep working on them and keep moving forward. Keep using your strengths, your positives, your skills, your general awesomeness and start again. The point is, you are going to begin again, and again, and again in life. In the words of Stevie Nicks: "in the web that is my own I begin again." It's not always easy but the more we replace the garbage with positivity, patience, perseverance, hard work, and determination, the more we nurture our spark into being.

SELF-LOVE FEELS BETTER

We decide what is deserving of our time and attention. We know what makes us feel safe, cared for, and loved. These become the building blocks of self-love. It takes practice to stand up to others, trust yourself and move through life's challenges. Once you start making decisions you know are right for you, you will feel a lightness to your being. It will feel easier inside. It can take time. It's important to be aware of how you grow and change during this process. You may be in a job that no longer feels right for you. You may realize you're in a relationship you've grown out of that was based on fears or patterns that no longer exist for you. These changes are normal and healthy.

FACING YOUR FEARS

It's not always easy to make these changes, to trust yourself, and face things that have caused you shame, fear, guilt, or sadness in the past. We generally let people walk all over us because we don't trust ourselves to ask for what we need to be happy and healthy. Past experiences and how you have felt in past situations may have taught you that you shouldn't speak up or ask for what you need. This is not true. It's a long-learned pattern that is incorrect, especially for women.

RELEASING SHAME

One of the ways to start trusting yourself is to release shame and guilt. When we release shame and guilt we become expansive creators in a vast universe that continues to open the more we let go of our old, incorrect thinking. Learn to scrub away the old erroneous stories you tell yourself. Shedding the skin of old perceptions about yourself allows you to step into a new perception and a new way of being. So much of that skin didn't start with you. Your shame, your parents' shame and layers and layers of ancestral fear, shame, guilt, and anger has been attaching itself to your generational being. This has created patterns that have existed for generations. Shed the skin, break the chains and start anew!

It's important to release old stories that tell you you are less than, incapable, not enough, etc.

HOW DO YOU SHED THE SHAME?

Sometimes there's crying in baseball. And it's awesome!

You shed those old perceptions through awareness. Looking at old patterns. Continuing to work on negative self-talk. Those negative thoughts and patterns came from a lot of this history. When you start to feel shame, guilt, or fear, STOP. Be present (I know it's scary). We generally try to get away from those feelings as fast as we can. Instead, be present, let the fear, shame, or guilt tell you a story. Let these feelings you push into the darkness tell you how hard it was to be there, what they need from you, and learn to accept these feelings and emotions for what they are, thank them and let them go.

We are humans, we are not perfect. It's ok to feel our feelings and accept the good, the bad and the ugly. The only person allowed to tell you which of these feelings goes in what category is you. Nobody is ever allowed to tell you your feelings are wrong, unworthy, or the ever famous "dramatic." Honor the scary places where you store all the unwanted parts of yourself. Sit with them, talk to them and release what no longer serves you as you work through them.

What you find here isn't going into any museum.

MOVING TO OUR CHAPTER JOURNALING PROMPTS

We are going to do a little more digging . . . ready?!?! Every being and creation on this planet has purpose and value. Every interaction we have with those beings and creations has purpose and value. Who are you in the world? How do you choose to interact with people and things? You're right, it constantly changes and evolves based on a lot of things. That evolution is good and it's important.

JOURNALING PROMPTS

In this section I've included some prompts to get us to start looking at our values, feelings, and experiences of self-love. Journal through any thoughts, memories, or experiences related to these concepts. You can tell stories and write down experiences you have had that make you who you are. Don't limit yourself to the questions here if you have more to say. You can go back to this over several days (or years) if you want. Remember you control your flow.

1. List five (or more) things that you really value. What things really matter to you? Why do each of these things matter to you in place of something else? Is honesty more important than kindness? Is bravery more important than loyalty? If you have a core set of things that you live by—what are they? Why did you choose some things over others? What experiences or people shaped the above answers? As an example, I have always been a person that has supported unions. I think they give workers the best chance to be safe, paid properly and not taken advantage of. My father grew up in the 1940's. It was post-depression; people were struggling for work and fearful they would be unable to house or feed their families. When my dad was in his teens he worked in a factory. His manager was a very kind person my father looked up to. He had children a little younger than my father. The man had been with this company for years.

Union organizers came in and really pressured employees to get on board to give them the best chance of success. My father's manager and co-worker was fearful this might cause him to lose his job and was worried about his family and didn't want to "rock the boat." The next day the man came into work and he had been severely beaten by those that wanted to start the union. The man would not speak about the incident but that experience impacted my father's image and ideas about unionization. These experiences throughout our lives color how we see, feel, and perceive the world around us. Have you had experiences that have formed or changed what you value?

2. What does your negative self-talk sound like? (Be specific) How long have you thought about yourself this way with the different words and things you say? Can you trace it back? What areas of your life have you developed negative self-talk around? (Looks, intelligence, perfection in all areas?) Take each negative word or phrase, write it down and across the page from it write down an opposite, positive statement and try to replace it daily every time you say the other one.

3. What is the difference between being lonely and being alone? Do you often feel lonely? Are there times when you are in a group of people and you feel lonely? Are you more introverted and you come alive when you are alone doing things that you love?

4. What is your greatest fear? Why?

5. What boundaries do you know you set well? What ones do you find yourself more uncomfortable with?

6. What does unconditional love look like? Can you recall a time when you cared for yourself unconditionally? Have you ever

loved anyone else unconditionally? Write about a time when you showed someone or something unconditional love and great compassion.

7. Try a little shadow work. Sit and bring up in your mind that time you expressed unconditional love to yourself or someone else. Keep that feeling in your mind. Then think of a time you were very hard on yourself or think of a part of yourself that causes you shame or embarrassment. Try to apply that feeling of compassion to that part of yourself you struggle with and don't want to look at. Spend some time with the feeling of unconditional love and caring before you bring in the other part. Try to have a loving, supportive, conversation with that part of yourself you struggle with. Ask that part of you about the pain it is in. Don't judge this part of yourself, just try to understand and accept any fear or shame and be loving with those feelings like you would if you were talking to a best friend that was having a horrible time. Write about that experience. Continue to practice that with various parts of yourself that you have outcasted.

8. Make a list of your accomplishments and achievements. Plan to make a list of them every time you feel down.

CREATIVE ACTIVITY

Okay! Now we are at the part of our chapter where we are going to use art to connect with our thoughts and feelings. If the last part was really hard this might be easier. There is NO wrong way to do art! Did you know that? It's true! You do not have to be an "artist" (whatever that means) for any of this. Go with your feelings and intuition and most of all, let go and have fun!

1. Grab a big piece of paper. Put some good music on, light a candle, whatever makes you happy.

2. Grab your favorite color in any medium: paint, markers, colored pencils, crayon, whatever works.

3. Sit down and take a deep breath. Let anything you are stressing about drift away. This is about having fun.

4. Take a photo of yourself that you have or use your phone and just snap one. Try to get a full body shot.

5. Print it. Cut it out and set it aside. If you are somewhere technology is limited just draw a basic body shape and cut it out.

6. On your big piece of paper use your paints or other materials and put your favorite colors all over the page. You can make shapes, marks, blotches, whatever appeals to you. Just have fun! Make it beautiful to your eye. Relax and enjoy the process. Let it dry.

7. Once you are done with your background, put your cut out where you want it on the page and glue it down.

8. Now, dress up that picture! You can add anything you want. You can put a crown on your head, put your pets by your side, give yourself wings, whatever you want. Add any colors you want, glitter, gel pens, cut out parts of magazines and add things. Create whatever image of yourself feels awesome to you.

9. Take a breath or a break.

10. Think about all the values and personality traits that have come up in this chapter. Write or type them on a piece of paper. Cut those words out and glue them all over the page. Voila! You're done.

Learning to love and accept who you are is a crucial part of your work on this planet. Nurturing and loving your precious little spark into being and sharing it with the world is a gift to the universe.

4
Journey to Connection

Things to Think About

Our relationships with others are one of the biggest things that happen to us on the planet. They require care and consideration.

Love and honor yourself when you invite someone into your life.

It is important to learn what you need in relationships and ask for it.

"Show me who you love and I will tell you who you are" Louisiana Créole proverb.

WHAT IS THE JOURNEY TO CONNECTION?

The journey to connection is about our connection to other human beings. These are some of the most powerful experiences we will have in our lifetime.

In this chapter, we are moving on from your individual journey to how you connect to other human beings. There are so many levels and layers to human relationships. It can be some of the most complex work we do during our earth walk. My goal for this chapter is to help you figure out what your relationships consist of, what you want out of them, and listening to and trusting yourself when you let other people into your life.

THE RANGE OF CONNECTION

Relationships have, at one time or another, taken us through the full range of emotions and the extremes of life's ups and downs. They have kept musicians and songwriters inspired for years! Relationships can range from acquaintances, friends, close friends, partners, spouses, bosses, co-workers . . . and yes parents, the complexity is endless.

Being connected to others in a meaningful way can provide great fulfillment in your life.

It is important to have a supportive network around you to help you feel validated, empowered, challenged and so many other things; and you have the opportunity to share life experiences with someone else who is doing the same thing.

It is important to have supportive people in your life that share and reflect and at times challenge your values. But as we learned from Michelle Obama in the last chapter, the work to get there has to come from within you. If one of our country's first ladies is still doing her personal work, I think we can all take a breath! Before we can find truly meaningful relationships in our lives we have to know who we are and what we have to offer to create relationships that are positive and meaningful.

DEVELOPMENT OF OURSELVES AND OUR RELATIONSHIPS

To understand how we get to where we are in the development of ourselves and consequently our relationships with others, I want to take a few minutes and share some things from Danish-German-American developmental psychologist and psychoanalyst, Erik Erikson.

He is known for his theory on psychological development through the human lifespan that is still used today. He lived from 1902–1994. I'm not going to write a big "to-do" on Erikson, but to provide understanding and a comparison of how people develop from a psycho-social standpoint tells us a bit about how and why they connect to others the way they do, or don't, or struggle in certain areas.

Forming Connections in Childhood

Erikson identifies the years of 0–1½ (in his theory) as the years of basic trust vs. mistrust. During this time, according to Erikson, if a child does not have consistency and stability, the impact can be multi-faceted. A child's ability to trust the world around them, transition into other relationships outside that of their parents, and see the world as logical and stable; or whether their perceptions will be one of fear of inconsistency and unpredictability, are all determined.

As we get older, Erikson's theory identifies 1½–3 years as the development of "Autonomy vs. Shame." If a child is encouraged and supported to explore the world around them they have a better chance of becoming more independent and self-confident. If they are discouraged they are more likely to experience and internalize a sense of shame, doubt and incompetence.

Adolescent Years

During the adolescent years, we grow into a phase of "identity vs. role confusion." According to Erikson's theory, during this time we are continually questioning. Who are we? What are our beliefs and goals? What are our values? What will our role be in life? How will we be different from those who raised us?

Moving into Adulthood

This blends into the first adult phase of Erikson's theory identified as "intimacy vs. isolation." This stage encompasses the development of intimate relationships and the safety, care and commitment to those adult relationships. How our ego develops in the earlier state of adolescence will impact how we handle and develop relationships as an adult.

Ego development and physical surroundings, at the earliest parts of our life, play a huge role in how we see the world around us.

HOW WE VIEW OUR CONNECTIONS

I am bringing up psychosocial theory in very broad strokes because it shows us how we form attachments and view connections to others. However, there is another piece to consider given our current day circumstances. In our current society, particularly here in the United States, these stages can be sped up, not focused on properly, or interrupted by traumatic events, changes in living circumstances, and many other occurrences.

Life, in our current circumstance, moves at a rapid and unpredictable pace. If we don't stop and figure out what we missed that has impacted us, our mental health and relationships can be adversely affected. We may not be aware of it, or want to deal with it, but it can impact our understanding of our identity, and our ability to connect, collaborate and form intimate bonds with others.

LEARNING TO LOOK AND UNDERSTAND

All we experience impacts how we think, feel, see, and understand the world around us.

What we can do is learn to look at it, know it's there, and understand why, at times, it might be affecting us.

When you think to yourself, "How did I get here? Why do I think the way I do about myself or others?" your initial relationships and environments are big pieces of it.

The disruptions, loss, void and lack of stability, as well as collective and individual trauma, can have an impact on how you answer the above questions. For example, if you are growing up in the current decade, the Covid pandemic, increase in school and public mass shootings, job loss, civil unrest, and large economic changes all impact your development and how you bond with others.

Our perception of the world around us and the people in it is always evolving. Is it the only thing that impacts us? NO! We are our own exceptional being that came into this universe with our own agendas and ideas, but it's important to look at and understand this part of our evolution.

CONNECTING AS WE GROW

When you are young, you see yourself through the eyes of the people, things, environments, and situations that are around you because you don't know any different yet. That's OK. You can't take on the world as a four-year-old.

Every human looks at the world through a different lens.

Each lens and each human is of their own making and experience. When you are young, you do not have the autonomy and understanding to control your world.

At this stage you are cared for by the people around you. Parental relationships are the longest and very often the most complex relationships in our lives. They can be tough as we get older and understand the world around us through our own lens.

If you have both parents in your life, it still can be tough. Many people struggle through divorce, losing a parent that has died, incarceration of a parent, or a parent that has left the family. There is a big hole labeled "Mom" or "Dad" that's filled with expectation, loss, and questions, in most cases. Even if we don't realize it on the surface, we may experience feelings of failure or inadequacy. These are feelings we may have, even when both parents are raising us and things seem fairly on track.

No matter what the circumstances of our nuclear family, we still have some idea, image, or experience of "parent." Sometimes it's a wonderful, joyful, supported experience with lots of great memories, and other times we are left with longing, sadness, and fear, but more often, it is all of those things mixed together.

Some of us have people that have raised us that are not "parents," and that's in here too. The relationships of those that raise us are important and when doing these exercises, deciding what relationships apply and how, is up to you. Take a minute to see what the image of "parent" or other relationships you had growing up, meant to you at the very start of your developmental journey.

CONNECTION DEEPENS THE MORE WE LEARN

As an infant, you just have images, vague impressions of smiles, kindness, meanness, happiness, fear, as you attempt to let those around you know if your needs are being met or unmet. You may have no memory of things involving your parents or caregivers, but it has an impact on you. Who is around you and what is happening when you are moving through many developmental stages during your younger life lays the groundwork for how you perceive and act in the world.

As we get older we have more of an ability to create and live through our own lens. We can see and honor our differences from others and understand they are there, but still stand in our own power. We learn to take the reins and decide who we will be. Those can be some very bumpy years no matter when they happen!

CONNECTION TAKES EFFORT

We need to work to communicate with others in ways that honor us and them. We can learn to ask for what we need. This is not a guarantee that it will happen. Communication with parents and loved ones can be troubled waters. Even though those close to you don't always hear what you are trying to communicate, you can still learn in these pages what's important to you and what you need to help you feel supported and ask for what you need.

Asking for what you need, as a way of taking care of yourself, is a skill that will benefit you for a lifetime.

Blaze that trail, girl!

How people respond teaches you a lot about them! People don't always honor it and can't or don't always understand what we are asking for, but it is important to know what we need for ourselves and ask for it.

If you picked this book up in your teen or college years you are doing it right now!!! That's great! You got this, girl!!! On the mysparkjourney.com website we have an inspiring women journaling section. Women like Greta Thunberg, and Amanda Gorman are some of the women that did their work and felt a calling at a very young age.

As for myself, I've always been exploring and studying all parts of the human experience, but I consider myself a late bloomer. It doesn't matter. What matters is doing the work, following your bliss and honoring your own path wherever and however you choose to blaze it.

CHOOSING YOUR CONNECTIONS

As we get older, our relationships go from being something we were born with to something we can choose. We start making friends. We have to manage bullies, haters, and eventually challenging co-workers that may be just as bad. How do we make decisions about who we want to align ourselves with and when we want to say enough?

Think about close friends you have or have had. What made you want to be friends with that person? How did they treat you? How did you treat them? It's important to find people that we share interests with, that treat us well and care about our general wellbeing.

BUILDING AND MAINTAINING IN THE YEARS OF BIG CHANGE

There is a lot of consideration when building and forming friendships. One of the hardest things about female friendships in your late teens and early twenties is how much people change. It is an important time of figuring out who you are, what you want in life, and the kind of people you want around you. In those years relationships can change on a dime and the outcome at times can be painful. One day you have a good friend that you have known for years, the next day . . . crickets. They won't even look at you.

Friendships in these years can be really stressful. It helps to stay focused on your own values and always have a short list in the back of your head (that we will create in journal prompts) of what is OK for you and what crosses a line in terms of how somebody treats you. Relationships can change so fast, it's important to always be looking at what's happening and how you feel about it even if you don't fully understand it.

Some things to remember when you are in relationships are:

1. Know what you want out of a particular relationship and try to understand what the other person wants. Do they match up?
2. Set clear boundaries with people so they know how to treat you.
3. Love yourself no matter what.
4. You can't change the past.
5. You can't change other people.
6. Learning from and moving out of a bad situation is one of the best gifts you can give yourself.
7. "The best way out is always through." —Robert Frost.

Friendships can be hard and hard work. They can also be totally worth the ups and downs.

EVERYBODY'S JOURNEY IS DIFFERENT

You blaze your own trail. Scary right? You are looking out over a huge expanse of land all overgrown with no trailhead in sight and the trail behind you has been all laid out. All you feel are inklings of things you want to change or do differently. Things you want to explore and develop. It is a challenging, scary, exciting, joyful, crazy time. Honor yourself, trust your feelings. If it feels like somebody is treating you badly, they most likely are. **"Your heart knows the way, run it that direction." —Rumi.** Your heart doesn't connect with pain, sadness, belittlement, or harm. It connects with joy, kindness, love, compassion, and understanding.

Trust yourself, you will notice very clearly people who may not be treating you so well. Remember, you are the one who is changing, some people will be used to the way they have always treated you and it is no longer OK. That's absolutely fine. It might be scary or difficult but it is important to set boundaries and ask for what you need in relationships.

JOURNALING PROMPTS

1. List five things that cause you pain, frustration or worry in a relationship you want to focus on: Examples: It hurts me when you call me _____. I know you aren't listening/ understanding me when you say or do _____.
Instead could you _____.
I get anxious when you scream. I feel angry or hurt when you swear at me. I feel belittled when you call me

   _____.

2. List things that you admire, learn from, or find loving about this same person. If that relationship is too painful, think of someone in your life that you can admire and count on for support and list these things about them.

3. List five traits you require in a friendship. Why?

4. List five traits that would be a friendship deal breaker. (Cruelty, dishonesty, etc..)

5. This next one is a doozie! Set some time aside in a place where you won't be disturbed. Take some nice deep breaths and begin.

   Use your journal or paper or whatever you choose. Favorite pens or writing utensils in your favorite colors may help. Put any items that make you feel happy, safe or supported by you; prayer beads, a rock you found that you love, or one of those little troll dolls. Whatever it is for YOU! This is your time and your process. Honor that process.

   In the following exercise I ask you to write letters to your mother and father. If you have not had any relationship in your life with either your mother or father, maybe you were raised by your grandparents or you have been in a group home a lot of your life, you can choose someone close to you that is a core relationship for you. Sometimes even though a mother or father is missing from our lives, that void requires conversation. If you have a lot to say to an absent parent, absolutely do that. It is your choice who you put in this activity below.

Write a letter to your mother. You never have to give it to her or show it to her or anybody else unless you choose. What do you want to say to her? Write as long as it takes. Write for as many sessions as it takes. Let it all flow out. Write what you are thankful for, happy about, sad about, and angry about. If you could say everything you need to say to her, what would it be? Don't censor yourself. Give this exercise as long as it needs. You may go back several different times, or you may be done on the first try. These core relationships unfold over a lifetime. If you are not going to share these letters, keep them in a very safe place. They are personal and deserve care and protection.

Do the same with your father or whoever is in that role that you know in your heart you need to write to. Who do you need to say something to?

There may be a flood of emotion with these letters. That's OK. Let your thoughts and feelings out. THEY ARE VALID!!! THEY ARE TRUE FOR YOU. THEY MATTER! HONOR YOURSELF. Take a deep breath. You did great! Pull a really good treat from the tool box! Giiirrrrlll maybe two!!! You earned it! Those big relationships are tough!

CREATIVE ACTIVITY

For this activity you are going to need a big sheet of paper, 8½" x 11" would be the smallest I would use. You need your favorite mediums again; paint, markers, crayons. You need a dark color sharpie marker. You can go as simple or as extreme as you want on any of these activities.

Start by cutting out the biggest heart you can out of your paper. Then you are going to use whatever type of line that appeals to you to section out the heart. Each section is a person you love in your life (pets can be in there also). Once you identify who these sections belong to, color the different spaces in your heart whatever colors remind you of the person going in that space. You can use old magazines and add other things like images or items that remind you of those you love. Whatever you want to add is fine, it is how your heart sees that person. Fill all your spaces for each person. You can also add a picture of them or write their name in their space. Let your activity dry. Take some deep breaths. You have mapped out part of your journey of connection. Nice job!!!

5
Warrior Soul

Things to Think About

When life is challenging, stay focused, stay curious. You got this. The storms will pass. Caring for yourself means building a network of support in your life in many different ways. Community, Identity, Stability. —Aldous Huxley

WHAT IS YOUR WARRIOR SOUL?

What is the warrior soul and why do you need warrior parts of yourself? This chapter is divided into two sections. The first part is your warrior armor, these are the things you do to keep yourself aware and protected and it also covers the opposite, the parts of yourself that may challenge you, or keep you from reaching the best part of yourself, and how those two things interact.

The next part of the chapter is our warrior community. These are the people around you that support your highest good and share the things that matter to you, and answer the question: why is it important to build that community?

Building and keeping connections to others is some of the most important work we do here on this planet. However, not everybody and everything is here to support us and help us find our path. We need to support and protect ourselves and find those who do want to share our path with us in a positive way. That's what this "Warrior Soul" chapter focuses on. Do we really need to approach things from a warrior standpoint? The answer is sometimes. Holding our boundaries and protecting ourselves, our spark, and those we love is thoughtful, careful, ongoing work.

I created the idea of warrior soul because to be a human on this planet, with all its challenges and battles, even the little day-to-day battles, you need to be a warrior. It helps you remain aware of what you want in life and how to honor that. You need to be a warrior to keep your spark alive.

You need to be a warrior to live your dreams.

You need to be a warrior so you don't let the devils of the world, or even the devils of the day, take your joy. That battle is warrior's work. You need to find ways to connect to your strength and joy. Call upon your courage, your independence, and trust in yourself. Those are the parts of yourself that can be vulnerable and need your protection.

Rally the troops!

FINDING OUR PEOPLE

We've spent the past few chapters figuring out how to nurture and protect our physical, mental, and emotional well-being. We examined who we are internally, what we want, how we want to be treated and how we will take care of ourselves. Now we want to look at how we protect all that? How do we protect the spark? The little embers that are meant for us, if nurtured and protected, can turn into a fierce bonfire that is our spark evolving. That spark will help us become who we are meant to be and what we are meant to share and leave to the world. How do we trust in it and help it grow? How do we find others like us? There are a lot of different little things we can do to continue to support our sparks.

In this chapter, we will talk about ways we can build our warrior's armor and our warrior cavalry. We will talk about who is in our tribe, why the tribe is important, and how to be discerning when you build your tribe and decide who you want as a supportive network in your life.

WHY DOES THE WARRIOR NEED ARMOR?

Another piece to this chapter will be about discussing two of the biggest dream stoppers and soul crushers out there: the emotions of fear and anger. When we select people to be around us and build our community, or we act on our own internal values and ideas, we ideally make decisions based on what we hope, but much more often we make decisions on what we fear.

Anytime you build a community around you, or work from thought patterns you have created over the years, you have to be clear about why you let certain people, things, or thoughts into your life. You want those reasons to be life-affirming and self-supporting, not coming from a place of scarcity, need, or lack.

FACING FEAR

Fear is one of the most common, pervasive emotions we face every day on many levels. We might be afraid we are not good enough, not pretty enough, or not smart enough, but it doesn't end there! There are loads of external fears, such as the fear of having medical issues, not having enough to eat, having a violent home, mass shootings, our car breaking down, and so many other things that can cause fear and anxiety on a constant basis that it's important to acknowledge it and keep it in check.

DON'T LET FEAR GUIDE YOU

When we are in that place of weakness that fear and anger can create, we don't always make the best decisions. Those are the times we can let people or circumstances in that do not serve our highest good. I think it is important to bring that idea front and center here because it is something we always need to stay focused on.

THE WARRIOR'S JOURNEY

There are internal and external things that happen to us that need warrior's help. What are the parts inside of us that need to be recognized? How can our warrior self help us battle our internal fear and anger and the external results that show up on our doorstep when we have not honored our best self. These negative influences can so quickly knock us off course and keep us from going forward, so we must be aware of them and learn how to handle them.

As you probably already know, volumes have been written about fear in our lives. For the purpose of this book, we want to look at what your greatest personal fear is and what types of smaller things might make you afraid or hold you back.

The warrior's journey is a lifelong pursuit.

FEAR IS DIFFERENT FOR WOMEN

Women can have different types of fears than males, especially during the teen years and early twenties. Psychologist Karl Abbrecht talks about fear in a couple ways that are useful to us as we do our work in this book. I'm going to share some of that with you. Dr. Albrecht talks about loss of autonomy, separation, and ego death. Sounds like a lot, right? Don't worry, I'm about to break it down for you.

LOSS OF AUTONOMY

Loss of autonomy has to do with not having control over your own existence; being restricted or cut off from your own decision-making ability. So, if you are in jail or a prisoner of war camp, you have loss of autonomy. It can be a physical restraint, an emotional one, or both. For example, if you are in a controlling relationship where you are not making your own decisions, you don't have autonomy. If you are in high school, living in your parent's house, and the latest battle with your parents has rendered you without a bedroom door—ding, ding, ding, you have lost your autonomy!

Whether you are the parent or teenager in this scenario, it is complex and difficult. There have been a handful of times over the years when a parent and child have come storming into my treatment room yelling at each other or not speaking at all. They came in with arms crossed, not looking at each other, with a list of battle plans and complaints. All of the pain, fear, anger and hurt on both sides is connected to the removed bedroom door. So losing control over what's happening in your life and your ability to make your own decisions is one type of lost autonomy.

SEPARATION IS PAINFUL

Another area that can cause us great fear is separation. Being kicked out of a group, being rejected, ignored by friends or groups can be very painful. All the mean things kids and adults do to one another can challenge our ability to trust ourselves. Being treated this way can cause a tremendous sense of fear. That fear can lead to making choices about the importance of being "in" even when it is to our great detriment. On the other hand, when we do choose to honor ourselves and deal with being excluded, the isolation and loss can also feel very difficult. We need to choose what's right for us even though neither thing may be perfect.

SHAME AND EMBARRASSMENT

The last fear I'm going to talk about from Dr. Albrecht is ego death. This has to do with humiliation, shame, embarrassment—things that can make you feel worthless. All these things happen on a big and small scale, sometimes on a day-to-day basis. A friend makes plans with your friend group and doesn't include you. A longtime friend makes up embarrassing things about you and tells your boyfriend in order to try to start dating him. You finally share your feelings with someone that you really, really like and they don't feel the same way. It can be so overwhelming that we shut down instead of moving forward.

STRENGTHEN YOUR WARRIOR SELF

That's why we need to create and strengthen our warrior self. We need to recognize what's happening and take charge of it. These things do not mean we are "less than." They do not change who we are as a person. Many of these things do not even belong to us. They may be about the other person's fears and choices. That's why it's so important to stay aware, hold our boundaries and be mindful of our own personhood.

MANAGING ANGER

The sister feeling to fear is anger. I say sister feeling because these two emotions have many of the same physical responses. Also, there are times when fear can lead us to anger. Anger can be an aggressive projection of our fear. Fear and anger are two of the most disruptive elements in our emotional repertoire. Anger is another emotion that can cause us to lose our way. As I said above, anger can often be an aggressive form of our fear. If we look at the example of the bedroom door, we might be in tears but we also might be furious, because our sense of power and sense of control is taken from us.

It quite possibly made you chuckle when you read the "door example," but if you have experienced it, maybe a very different feeling comes to mind. Think about other times you may have had those same feelings in an office with a brutal co-worker, dealing with a belittling client or boss. Same monkey, different circus.

DON'T LET ANGER TAKE YOUR SPARKLE

Anger is another emotion you experience that can take time, energy and achievement away from you, especially when you let it fester and control you. When you get so caught up in things that don't help you, it stops you from fulfilling your purpose. It is important to be mindful of how you are experiencing your anger and fear, and how much of your life it is taking up and for how long.

The Buddha said, "Holding onto anger is like drinking poison every day and expecting the other person to die."

BUILDING YOUR WARRIOR SELF

So how do we build and nurture our warrior self through times of fear and anger? What are some skills we can use to help us?

1. Experience your emotions, feel them, accept and honor them for what they are, knowing it's okay to be angry and afraid at times, and as you are able, move past them.

2. Remind yourself that the world is bigger than a particular situation. Your warrior self is here to help you battle the hard stuff and lift you up over the fray.

3. Remind yourself of your accomplishments and achievements, and how special you are.

4. Always try to stay joyful and keep your humor handy.

5. Stay in a place of gratitude.

6. Pull out your tool kit from Chapter Two and use some of the strategies to move out of a negative headspace.

We need to stay in a state of awareness of the work we need to do as situations arise. We have the knowledge and power to do it but it takes practice and perseverance.

OUR EXTERNAL WARRIORS

The next part of this chapter is about our external warriors. They are the people around us who have drifted across our life in some way. Who do you admire in the world? Who do you look up to? Who lifts you up when you are down? The person can be living or dead. Your cavalry can be fictional characters, religious figures, political figures, creators, activists, anybody you look up to. Who are the people you admire that have been through really tough things yet persevered? They can also pop up out of the blue and be a real flesh and blood human. Our warrior clan can be many things.

Julie and the Barista

I have a friend Julie who was talking to her favorite barista at Starbucks. She learned that he was a painter and at times did summer camps with kids learning how to understand and express their feelings and emotions through art and painting. They got together and started a non-profit for kids that had been through trauma, to use art as one of their healing tools. You start talking, take a risk and put yourself out there, and you never know who might be in your tribe.

BUILD YOUR CAVALRY

In a very material world, where there are continual ethical challenges and decisions to be made about protecting our dreams and the dreams of others, we need help. We need our cavalry. We need people that have gone through a lot and come out the other side, that we can look to for support and guidance. This is a reminder to keep images, people, and support around you that remind you to stay strong and focused on your dreams and your spark. The importance of staying curious all your life, not giving in to your emotions, and looking to others who have accomplished their life goals, is very helpful in staying strong and honoring your warrior soul. We are talking about heroes and icons that we look up to that can lead us along our path and support us when things get tough.

WHO ARE YOUR HEROES AND WARRIORS

I know I've mentioned some heroes and heroines already but some examples are: Sojourner Truth, Malala Yousafzai, Greta Thunberg, Katniss, Rey from Star Wars, Hermione Granger, and Frida Kahlo. The list of heroes, both fiction and nonfiction, is endless . . .

These are people we don't know personally but they shine a beacon of hope into the world and whatever beacon you resonate with is how you choose your warriors.

ARCHETYPES

Warriors can be people that we admire in our life. They can be archetypal characters that we invent from our psyche. According to Swiss psychiatrist Carl Jung, archetypes are repeating images, patterns or ideas that repeat in all the universal subconscious. They exist in every culture throughout the world.

We aren't getting too far into the works of Carl Jung, but if you are interested there will be resources on mysparkjourney.com. The point is, there are concepts or images that we relate to or resonate with when we see or hear them. The mother or father archetypes are some of the most popular that everyone across the world recognizes. The warrior archetype is another recognizable one. Hence, part of the inspiration for this chapter.

Archetypes are primordial images that reflect basic patterns that are common to us all, and which have existed universally since the dawn of time."
—Carl Jung

FIND THINGS THAT MAKE YOU FEEL SUPPORTED

We all have things that we personally resonate with that can help us feel supported at various times and help support us in very specific ways. These are universal but they are also very personal and it can be really fun and helpful to identify them and have them around us.

You are not in this alone. Life offers a lot of opportunity for growth, excitement and connection. In the words of Shawn Mendes, describing people's connection to each other, from the song "Believe," "It's a wild and beautiful fire and I believe in you." Who knows where your inspiration comes from. Find out! It's fun and inspiring.

We Built a Warrior Wall

When I was in my twenties, I worked as an Occupational Therapy Assistant running groups on an adolescent psychiatric unit. The kids were going through so many things. Some were coming from correctional facilities, some were coming from very horrific home situations, and some were really struggling with depression or anxiety. I always tried to stay present with them. A lot of the patients were angry, sad, and terrified. They would taunt me and each other. They would shut down and refused to speak or were constantly in tears. That kind of crisis is very difficult and they were going through it in front of a lot of other people.

As somebody trying to be present for them, hold space, and provide a sense of connection and teach useful skills for managing that struggle, it felt quite overwhelming at times. Sometimes it felt like I couldn't help at all.

One of those days I decided to make a warrior wall in my apartment. I made a wall of women that were, or had, accomplished things, and inspired or helped others. Madeleine Albright (the first female Secretary of State in the US) was there, Sojourner Truth was there, Joan of Arc was there, and my favorite heavy metal singer, Doro Pesch was there. I filled it with women that were breaking barriers and boundaries, fighting for what was right and fighting to make things better.

WHO INSPIRES YOU?

These women always inspire me and help me to focus on what's important when I'm feeling overwhelmed. They made me feel strong and empowered. They made me understand what a gift it was to work on this unit and how important it is to listen to each other, to listen to every story and hardship, and work together. It helped me bring to the unit the idea that we can keep trying to move forward, even when the circumstances have been so dire and horrible, and the evidence doesn't appear to support the idea that things will change and get better.

After creating my wall of heroines and heroes, I brought stacks of magazines and pictures to the unit. I suggested to the patients that we build a collective wall of warriors and do the same thing I had done.

Some kids laughed or scoffed or flat out refused. Some were happy to give it a try. I told everybody they didn't have to do it in a group, they could add people on their own and didn't have to talk about it. Slowly over the next week or so people started appearing on the warrior wall. We had Sailor Moon, Erykah Badu, Geronimo, Lil Wayne, Oprah, Dobby, and Nurse Linda—one of the only nurses that wasn't mean to everybody. The wall, over time, had a vibe all its own. It was a place of connection, conversation, and laughter. I noticed it was one place where the kids were never mean to each other. They let each other's heroes and heroines be who they were.

Who are your heroes that make you feel like that? This can be an important practice for all of us. Who are your warriors?

WE ALL NEED A FAIRY GRANDMA?

Sometimes who is able to help you will surprise you. I had a young client that I worked with on a psychiatric unit in Colorado (I moved around a lot). I met her and worked with her when she was in her teens. She had suffered a tremendous amount of physical, sexual and emotional abuse through her life. When she was small she did not have anybody to trust. She was not raised in any particular religious tradition and had no faith to lean on. During her very chaotic, abusive childhood, at a time when things were particularly terrifying, she created Fairy Grandma. Fairy Grandma was a fairy type figure with giant wings and wispy branches for hair and a very kind face. It was an entity she created in her imagination that she prayed to, talked to, and asked for help from, to take care of her when she was afraid.

We all need to have a Fairy Grandma in one way or another. We need to build a collection of guardians and protectors, that are very important to us, both living and not, real and imaginary, that support us on our journey. We will also talk about this in the "North Star" chapter. In this chapter we are talking about people we might look to for support, who have done incredible things in the world, or admire what they have accomplished.

CONNECTING TO YOUR WARRIOR SOUL

When I became a therapist, I started my own practice. It was a very intense time. I spent hours in coffee shops writing client forms and HIPAA forms, researching, looking for an office, filling out reams of application papers and contracts to become a provider for various insurance companies, and all kinds of scary stuff.

During that time, I tapped into people that represented the warrior archetype to me, and again kept positive images around me to bring support, such as Joan of Arc, and Georgia O'Keefe. I listened to a lot of heavy metal music because it gives me strength, and exciting energy. I had a charm of Archangel Michael around my neck because he was a fighter for truth and justice and I really wanted to help people. My friend Beverly and I would walk and talk through the "hows" and "whys" of what was to come in the gorgeous forests near my home.

DON'T LET YOUR DOUBTS THROW YOU

There were a lot of times I doubted myself and thought, "you're making a big, expensive mistake right now—you can't do it." So not only do we sometimes need to protect ourselves from people that don't believe in our path, but we need protection from our own doubts and to be able to trust ourselves when we are not so sure.

It was a bumpy road in the beginning of my practice. I was working full time outside of my practice and using my income to pay rent on an office, in addition to a mortgage. Internet, website, and marketing costs along with all kinds of different things soaked up a lot of money in the beginning when there really wasn't much coming in. Battling insurance companies, filling out claim forms incorrectly, learning one system after another with no money coming in was very anxiety provoking, but eventually things smoothed out.

WHAT YOU LOVE IS MORE IMPORTANT THAN WHAT YOU FEAR

On the other side of that, I absolutely love being a therapist. I wanted to do it on my own instead of working for somebody else so I could work with the clients I felt I could be most useful to. If I needed to waive a fee for a family that was really struggling that was my decision. I could make my own hours and run my business how I wanted it run.

The first year that I broke even with my business I remember crying in my accountant's office. He was used to tears, but these were good tears! I've always had anxiety around money, so starting a business was a really big step for me on many levels.

It's so important to learn to trust yourself and stick by yourself and keep doing your personal work along with all the other work you are responsible for. Personal work is just as important.

Sometimes it's worth the battle to stay in a project, sometimes it's ok to pull out of situations not meant for you. Just trust yourself and continue to explore your thoughts and feelings and honor the answers you get from yourself.

LEARNING TO TRUST YOURSELF

When you trust in your own strength and allow yourself to be lifted up by everyone and everything that believes in you, it can move you forward instead of dragging you down. You can create certain elements in your life that can help you feel joyful, strong, supported and remind you who you are.

KEEP BUILDING AND DREAMING

Build your dreams and work on your goals around people you gravitate towards. Things that ground you, like regular self-care routines, or certain people who help you breathe easier when you are near them. Also, make things that support you, and build up part of your warrior's armor. What are those things? Your faith, cultural traditions, how you relate to others, and building a sense of belonging and purpose creates your warrior during your life on Earth. In building these things up around you, you are building your own personal mythology.

Do these things sound like some of the things that we used to ward off fear and anger? They are. Does this sound similar to things that might be in your tool kit? They are. All the things we do to care for ourselves, build our armor and show ourselves love and compassion will show up in the many intersections of our lives that need care and support.

A Woman's Story

As dedicated to your path as you might be, it is not always easy to live your dreams and goals. I worked with an incredible young woman who I'll call Claire. When Claire started college she was really active in political and social justice causes. Since she was a child she was always called to situations she felt were unjust. She didn't like seeing people mistreated and she had a lot of anger and passion drawing her to causes she felt she could help with.

Claire worked for animal rights. Claire helped build her local LGBTQIA+ chapter by working a lot of festival booths, handing out materials and running chapter meetings. Claire was a tremendous help to the causes she served but this work and community also helped Claire feel strong and connected. Finding her community of people and fighting for things she felt very passionate about empowered Claire. Growing up, Claire struggled with depression, and at times, low self-esteem.

As a gay woman, Claire struggled in high school to find her community and it caused further isolation, pain and sadness. Claire continued to persist through all her struggles, even though at times it was very overwhelming. She slowly learned to honor and care for herself even when others didn't agree and learned the importance of honoring and trusting herself for who she was.

Claire was raised in a family that had extremely different values and etiologies than she came to believe as she got older. She and her parents really struggled to see and validate each other. Because Claire's family circle had such different views, they struggled to support her and that non-existence of validation and support was very isolating and painful for Claire.

FIND PEOPLE THAT SHARE YOUR BELIEFS

The need for support from people that share your belief system is one of the many reasons it's important to find your circle, and your warriors, that help you feel validated and empowered in who you are. That doesn't mean the relationships with people that struggle to understand you aren't important, but learning to love and accept who you are is crucial. Loving and accepting yourself just as you are, your special spark, that you came into the world with, is your gift to the universe.

Playing small doesn't serve anybody. You need to be who and what you are in the strongest way possible. If that strength is being soft spoken and kind, or as passionate and loud as a lion, it matters that you express it. Claire was able to engage her dreams and passions and helped other people do the same.

When Claire engages in her relationship with her parents she does it from a place of validation and love for herself and them. It's hard to be different when you're doing it by yourself and people don't agree with you (especially parents!) but it's important to find your way, your voice, and the love to honor who you are meant to be.

JOURNALING PROMPTS

1. List five things that make you angry.
2. List five things you do to manage your anger in a healthy way.
3. What is your greatest fear?
4. List five things you do to support yourself when you feel afraid.
5. When did the members of your cavalry come into your life and how have they changed over time?
6. What values do you associate with each cavalry member?
7. What have they taught you about acceptance and connection?

CREATIVE ACTIVITY

In this chapter activity, we are going to create the "warrior cavalry" we have been talking about. In this exercise we will need paper, glue, access to the internet if you have it, and your favorite medium, like paint, markers, etc. Gather pictures of who you want on your cavalry page. You can look on Google, Pinterest, or magazines. You can also just make pieces of paper with their names on them and decorate each piece of paper with colors and images that remind you of that person.

First, take a piece of paper and color the background. Use colors that represent strength and protection to you. You can also use stamps or stencils if you have them to add additional interest and imagery. Relax, have fun and take your time doing your background. Remember, you cannot do art wrong. Think about what you have learned in this chapter.

After your background is complete and you have let it dry, start adding (gluing in) the warriors you have chosen. If they have famous phrases you want to add next to them go ahead and do that. Lay out your cavalry however it feels right to you. And voila! You've assembled your cavalry. If you want to work along with me on this activity there is a video at mysparkjourney.com.

You can place this collection of supporters somewhere you can see it when you need it. You can place your cavalry on a bedroom wall, or a closet door. It can be there to remind you what makes you strong and help you remember to take care of yourself.

6
North Star

Things to Think About

"We are not human beings having a spiritual experience. We are spiritual beings having a human experience." —Pierre Teilhard de Chardin

"Sometimes I think that there are only two instructions we need to follow, to develop and deepen your spiritual life; to slow down and let go." —Oriah Mountain Dreamer

"The privilege of a lifetime is to become who you really are." —Carl Jung

YOUR SPIRITUAL SELF

Welcome to the north star. What is the north star and this chapter about? The soul. Our spiritual selves and our spiritual path. Our north star is our core being, our soul energy. Our soul is our interface between the physical and spiritual. If we can stay connected to our soul, our life force, our love force, we can create and live the life we were meant to live. We can weather storms and stay in a state of grace and gratitude through our connection to the divine.

Spiritual practice gives you that connection. That connection sustains you, comforts you, and nurtures you. No one can steal it, take it from you, beat it out of you, no matter the circumstances. That connection, in the words of Tina Turner, is "beyond." Many Buddhists and Sufi practitioners and even John Lennon believed that love is all that exists in the world and you are the vehicle for that love. Everything else is an illusion. Your soul, your spiritual self, is the connection to that divine love force. So in the words of Madonna . . . "What are you gonna do?" You can exist without any spiritual connection or you can go for it.

YOU, THOSE AROUND YOU, THE WIDER COMMUNITY, THE UNIVERSE

Up until this point we have focused on the physical and material things in our lives. We have worked on relationships with others. We have looked at our internal values and needs and wants. We learned about standing up for who you are and finding your tribe. This chapter is about the journey of the spirit. This journey is outside of your individual, beautiful self. Connection to spirit is larger than anything in your day-to-day life and it can help you step back and see a larger existence. There are lots of things to consider. Let's get to it.

ALL THINGS IN THE UNIVERSE ARE CONNECTED

In this chapter, you will look at the north star within you. Once you lift out of your day-to-day battles, connections, and trappings, you engage with something bigger.

Connecting with spirit, with God, with the divine, with pure love, is why we pray, meditate, chant, etc. Spiritual practices and beliefs balance and center you.

Spiritual practice quiets the mind so the heart can see.

The spiritual practice you bring into your life is your heart's language for connecting to the Source, to God—to something bigger than yourself.

This connection reminds us that we are all part of each other, and part of the Source. The whole universe and all that is in it is connected.

This life force flows through all things: humans, plants, animals, minerals, mountains, oceans. It has an energy and an existence that connects us all together. We choose what we believe about that life force, how we interact with it, how we treat it, how we care for it on a daily and life-long basis.

CONNECTING IS NOT ALWAYS EASY

Accepting that we are all part of each other is not always an easy task. Somebody cuts you off in traffic. Perhaps a friend or co-worker talks about you behind your back, or when someone you know has very different political beliefs, values, and ideas about how the world should be, it can be hard to not feel distance between yourself and others. It's hard to look that person in the face and say, "that's me, we are all the same, we are all part of each other."

Instead, we feel separate, even pulling ourselves away because we are hurt or angry.

The struggle of separation exists on an individual, community, national, and global level.

The pain of how we treat and mistreat each other exists anywhere there are human beings.

WHAT IS YOUR SPIRITUAL PATH?

Maybe you have no spiritual or philosophical practice and have never considered this area of your existence or found value in it. Perhaps you have been raised with very devout practices that you are steadfast in and that anchor your life. It's possible you were raised in a certain tradition and now that you are older and are learning and understanding the world differently, you feel uncertain about what you have learned, or you have found a whole new path altogether.

When you look around at the religious structures or dogmatic doctrine and you see holy wars and genocide and pain and suffering as a result of some beliefs, both religious and political, it can cause you to wonder, "What is going on?!" The path you are on is divine and beautiful and meant for you at this time. Still, it's important to examine what you believe. It's important to look at how what we believe and how we behave impacts others and ourselves.

THERE ARE MANY PATHS TO SPIRIT

What is your spiritual background? Do you practice Christianity, Buddhism, Islam,

Judaism, Wicca, Hindu, Baha'i, Shinto, Indigenous American spirituality, Indigenous African spirituality, Gnosticism? How did you develop your spiritual path?

There are so many beautiful, exquisite, graceful religious paths that have existed over the history of the human race spanning tens of thousands of years or longer—we are still digging right? The Buddha said, "all rivers lead to the ocean." Love leads back to love. I believe love is the strongest force there is. What do you believe? What has been your experience with love and connecting to spirit? Have you thought about that idea before or experienced it in some way that comes to mind?

WHO ARE YOUR TEACHERS?

We have had rare and precious teachers throughout history that have helped us, taught us, nurtured and loved us—The Buddha, Jesus Christ, Mohammad, to name a few. One might say if your path is based in love, compassion, and kindness, then it is true. What do you feel connected to? What brings you to your true self? We are going to take some time and look at your beliefs, your experiences, your questions, your needs, your goals and the path forward for this part of your existence.

HOW DID YOU GET HERE?

You have been developing your beliefs your whole life and many spiritual teachers say even before you were born. Whether you were raised with a spiritual tradition, or not at all, your vast experiences have woven a tapestry of belief within you. How do you want to take that experience forward?

Your heart and soul are working together to give you the clarity to get through times of difficulty and treasure life's sacred and precious moments. Some of the most important things you can know in this life is that you are part of the divine, you are loved, you are enough, you are precious, you are stardust.

My Own Journey

My own journey was constantly developing. As a young child I was raised in a small Christian church. I have very happy memories of that time. People were very kind, I felt a very strong connection to Jesus. I was comforted by the stories and felt very at peace when I prayed. I felt very connected when I prayed. I remember sitting in the dark sanctuary when my parents were finishing various duties or at choir practice and it was just bliss. The silence, the light flowing through the stained glass gave a tremendous sense of peace and connection.

While I feel that support has never left me, as I got older, I began to change. I struggled with large parts of the Christian faith that didn't accept different types of people into their fold. People that were gay or lesbian, or people that had substance problems weren't always welcome. Women could not hold many positions, and the numerous abuse scandals made me question my beliefs. So many people are described as sinful and unacceptable. So, I began to question what I grew up learning. I was angry, sad, and hurt, but more than that I felt a need to grow. I spent many hours at the library reading things on spirituality. I read books by Carl Jung, among others. I took comparative religion and philosophy. I wanted to know what it is that connects us all. I knew that there wasn't just one answer. People of many faiths work together for the greater good. At the same time, people continue to shut each other out and condemn each other.

Looking Deeper Can Be Painful. That's OK.

For a long time it made me angry. I was not practicing any faith and was more interested in politics and philosophy and the study of various traditions. I focused on the Earth, reading Walt Whitman and Ralph Waldo Emerson. I learned nature-based ritual, practicing Wicca for a time. I met my amazing friend Christine when we worked together at a psychiatric hospital in Tucson and she introduced me to Buddhism and the teaching of Nichiren Daishonin. We chanted together; I was welcomed into people's homes to chant, study and talk about Buddhism and Soka Gakkai (SGI) and the work that they do all over the world. For ten years steadily, I practiced Buddhism and deepened my understanding of compassion and kindness and giving to others. But again, there was a need to grow. And a part of me missed the "personal connection" of Christianity.

I worked with the archangels and saints. I studied the dimensions and interconnectedness of all beings through reading Rudolph Steiner and Helena Blavatsky. I studied Shamanism, both east and west, and I read about so many incredible lives of those who have struggled and sacrificed to bring compassion, love and teaching throughout the world. I will study the spiritual nature of myself and humans for the rest of my life. I will always be growing in spirit. My hope is that my path will always be moving forward. For myself, love, compassion, kindness, and creativity inspire me and move me forward and hold me steady.

ELEMENTS OF CHOOSING OUR PATH

Connecting to your true, spiritual self can take many different paths. As we have talked about in earlier chapters, there are as many paths as there are people. Some of you have had many twists and turns in your spiritual path due to divorce, abuse, substance use in families, war, migration, and many other unexpected traumas that change us. Those experiences can bring us closer to God, closer to the divine.

Traumatic experiences of loss and pain can teach us the importance of connecting with something bigger than ourselves. Those experiences can also pull us away from God and our spiritual selves when we struggle to understand or wrap our head around difficult things that have happened or that we have witnessed. Those that perpetrate violence and abuse others have lost their connection to spirit. It can be a difficult path to regain if you have been continually abused or corrupted by things that are the antithesis of connection to the divine.

"Knowing your own darkness is the best method for dealing with the darkness of other people." —Carl Jung

Things will always change and evolve and it's important to experience that growth and manage the ebb and flow of your life. Your spiritual and philosophical beliefs are an extremely important part of managing that ebb and flow and it gives you the strength and guidance to go forward. Your beliefs will support you in ways that can be crucial to your growth. Honoring your beliefs helps you to reach your goals, heal from pain and loss and gives you the ability to stay resilient. A daily practice you develop in this chapter can provide that support.

THE HEART CONNECTION

Most people have heard the term "you know in your heart." That heart connection, that feeling of support from within, is something you start to develop as a child and continue to understand and develop as life goes on. I have worked with so many young people who do not have that connection within them. They feel lost, unsure, or untrusting of what is within them. Not having an external point of reference bigger than yourself, and an understanding that we are all connected, can be a barrier to growth and make it hard to have resilience in difficult times.

So many young women have been told not to trust themselves. Whether it is a boss, a parent, a significant other, a workplace, or a government agency, our culture has told women for a very long time that someone else should be making decisions for them. They end up not trusting their heart's center, their soul's knowing. The truth is you need to trust your intuition. You need to know you are worthy, and important, and a gift to the world. Your heart's knowing, even if you are still figuring it out, is what matters. **It's who you are!**

Trusting your heart center, your true north star, will help you stay focused when people disagree with you, but there is something you need to say or do in your life. Learning what your north star is and to trust it will help you when somebody close to you turns against you. When you suffer a loss, are not sure what is next in your life, or what your purpose is, you need your north star. That north star, that center of us, which steadies us and guides us, is what we will identify, build, or remember in this chapter.

"The divine is revealing itself to us every day. All we have to do is pay attention."
—Andrew Pacholyk

IT'S ALWAYS IMPORTANT TO STAY CONNECTED

It is important to stay connected to your north star. That connection provides a bigger, broader view of your existence. Working through your journaling prompts at the end of this chapter can help you build and support that connection. It's bigger than any one life situation and your north star, your soul center, is where you go when you are feeling unsteady.

Is it only in times of survival and struggle that we need our north star? Heck no! We can use it to reach our goals, to trust ourselves to change paths in life, to follow our dreams, to tell the world who we are! Even if we think we do not have a particularly spiritual path, our passion, and our love for what's important to us in the world is a representation of our north star.

One Man's Story

When I was in my twenties, I worked as a hospice volunteer. I sat with people who were dying, read to them, listened to music with them, and even held their hands while they slept if they asked me to. To become a volunteer at the time you went through a forty-hour training and you heard many stories from nurses and clergy and others that cared for the dying.

The common understanding in hospice, which was witnessed again and again by caregivers, was that when someone dies they have a "package" that comes for them. It's family, it's angels, it's their favorite religious hero. Somebody comes to help them over the bridge, through the tunnel of the tremendous white light or through the veil. What all my research and talks with the amazing people that do hospice care tells me is that it all varies depending on your beliefs.

I was sitting with a man who was a scientist his whole life. He was extremely kind, gentle, and funny. He didn't have any close family that I saw when I was on the shift and he didn't have any pictures or personal effects that suggested otherwise. We would talk often and he didn't have any particular religious beliefs.

He was very open and we would talk about what his "package" might look like. Would he get one? He asked a lot of questions about what others experienced during this time. His main area of study during his career was birds. He loved birds and knew more about birds than I could ever think to ask about them. Birds were his true love and passion.

When he finally passed he had been in and out of consciousness for a few days on pain medication, mostly morphine. I could see in his face that it was time and I noticed he was looking at something in the distance. He was very weak and it was very hard to understand him. I sat near with my hand on his and was just present.

All of a sudden he laughed very softly with slight amazement and joy, "It's a purple crane . . . it's flying ahead . . . it wants me to follow." I rubbed the back of his hand with my thumb and smiled and he was gone shortly after. The world is such a massively incredible place with more possibilities, joy, love, and grace than we can ever fathom.

It's important that we figure out what our spiritual gifts, involvement, responses and engagement will be for ourselves. These choices change and evolve as we do; it's not always easy, but so important to look at.

CONNECTING TO YOUR SPIRITUAL PATH NOURISHES YOU

This inner work is an important part of balancing our body, mind, and spirit and living life on a path of holistic self-care and self-love that we can share with others.

There are many times in life when we feel like we are swirling around off our mark. We are anxious, depressed, our mind is racing, and things are not connecting. We failed a test, lost a job, broke up with somebody, someone is ill, and it feels like things around us start to spin out of control and we are no longer sure of ourselves. When these situations start to happen and you spin into thoughts of the future or regrets of the past and worry about this or that happening, you start creating things in your mind that haven't happened yet and just spin like crazy. We need to . . . STOP! Stay present. Your north star is within you. During these times we need to stay connected to where our spirit lives and where our heart feels safe.

CONNECTING EVERYTHING SO FAR

Before we start the journal prompts for this chapter, we are going to look at our overall purpose . . . again! Once you start doing your personal work, the world and your relationships and perceptions start to change. At the beginning of this book you started looking at yourself, you expanded to encompass your relationships, you expanded to your larger community and then to your connection with the universe and God. As you do that things become clearer. You become more discerning in what you want in your life and what you don't and then the things you want start springing up like the geysers at Yellowstone! They become more visible and obvious to you. You are able to start living a more genuine, stable, creative existence based on your own spark essence. This is just the beginning.

JOURNALING PROMPTS

1. What are your religious beliefs or spiritual practices?
2. How do those beliefs show up in your everyday life? In what way do they inform how you interact with people?
3. Do you want more spiritual practice and study in your life?
4. Has your belief structure changed since you have gotten older? Have you questioned what you believe or changed your spiritual path?

5. How much a part of your life do you want your spiritual practice to be? How much is it a part of your life now? Is there a difference?

6. What makes you feel connected to spirit? Do you have times where you stop and connect to spirit regularly?

7. Do you have goals for your spiritual life and how it is part of your existence? Write them here. You can write action steps if you know them.

CREATIVE ACTIVITY

For our creative activity we are going to make a north star bracelet to remind us of what is important to us and connect to spirit to feel supported. There are several ways we can do this but I'm going to lay out the simplest one here. If you want to work along with me you can go to mysparkjouney.com.

For this activity we need a 12" piece of elastic cord. It should be thin enough for the beads you have chosen to go through. Next you need sixteen smaller beads around 5-6 mm, and four larger beads around 8-9 mm that you will string as every 5th bead. You can use beads you already have, get beads at a local craft store or go to a second hand store and get a piece of jewelry with beads you like and repurpose it. This bracelet is to help you feel connected to spirit or God throughout the day and there are many different ways you can use it to connect to spirit that we will talk about after we make our bracelet.

To start, lay out your elastic cord in front of you. Take one end and lay a 4" piece of string perpendicular to your elastic string with two inches on each side. Use your elastic cord and tie that to the string on the end of your elastic cord. Leave a 1–2 inch tail of elastic as you tie your thread on. This will keep your beads from slipping off as you string them and you can add charms or extra beads on at the end. The extra tail of elastic we are going to use to tie the bracelet together. Once that is complete slip one of the big beads on all the way to the end of your elastic cord. Then string four smaller beads. Next add another big bead. Continue with this pattern until all your beads are strung. When you are done make sure the bracelet fits your wrist to the length you want before you tie it. Once you know how long you want the bracelet, tie both ends of the elastic together. If you would like to add extra charms or beads of symbols that represent your faith on the thread you can string them and tie the ends.

Wearing this bracelet can remind you of our connection to spirit. You can think of a positive phrase you use in your spiritual practice and say it as you touch each bead. You can pray for someone you are worried about as you touch each bead. You can say things you are thankful for as you touch each bead. You can use the beads in each section to pray and be thankful for something different. If you have a current spiritual practice, that might guide you to how you want to interact with your bracelet. You can remind yourself of your spiritual goals as you touch each bead. There are many ways to use this bracelet for prayer, support or spiritual work. Mostly it can just be there to support you and help you feel closer to the divine. Enjoy!

7
The Spark Wrap Up

Things to Think About

Your individual spark is divinity in motion.

Creating the tools and doing the work is essential.

Love yourself first and everything else will fall into place in time.

True human connection is an incredible and important teacher.

Together we can do so much.

Stay connected to the Divine, and your spark will always sparkle!

THE ALPHA AND THE OMEGA (THE BEGINNING AND THE END)

Here we are. At the end of the workbook and also the beginning of an amazing journey. We have covered so many things. We have investigated ideas, thoughts, feelings, insights, pains, joys, goals, truths and so much more. There were a lot of big things crammed into a little space and time, but this is just the jumping off point. The question at this point is, "What do I take forward?" That's what this chapter is about.

This last chapter is for reviewing all we've discovered, and thinking about how you will take it forward. You are on the warrior's path to finding your true spark! Understand that what you found is precious. What stood out to you, what resonated with you, are parts of yourself that deserve cultivation and care as you move forward. The work you did here is something to be honored and cherished. You are transforming and growing into your true self.

A QUICK CHECK IN

You did great! You discovered, you achieved, you brainstormed, you explored, and look at all that you found! Take a moment and think of three quick things that you learned or achieved in these pages. Next, think of three action steps you're going to take to continue your journey. What areas will you be working on? You can always go back to the chapter or spruce up the strategies in your tool kit when you've seen what's still working and what isn't. Your daily practices, coping strategies, physical care plans and sources of inspiration are all organic and ever-changing, just like you. The information you have discovered in this book can help you on your unfolding path to the rest of your life.

Chapter 2 Rewind

In Chapter 2, you created your building blocks for a healthy life. Learning to support yourself, cope with difficulties and honor your needs, is a crucial piece to an amazing existence. You created and examined wholeness strategies in the areas of relaxing your mind, body, and brain. You learned about the importance of using humor and engaging in the community around you to build hope and strength within you, providing wellness and relaxation as a result.

Chapter 3 Rewind

In Chapter 3, you examined yourself and different ways you might manage your internal awareness. We talked about the practice of self-love, boundaries, negative self-talk, releasing shame, and learning to accept that we are the light and the shadow. You have identified a skill set to care for yourself and your beliefs. You can continue to use the exercises you completed in this chapter.

When you think about the "Self-Love" chapter, how much has changed for you? Did you change any of the ways you care for yourself? Did you notice any boundaries in your relationships that may need some tweaking?

The more you understand what self-love means to you, and deepen your practice with it, the more you will feel balanced and grounded. Combining that practice with truly loving who you are brings together all the other pieces of your life, relationships, and spiritual practice. When that happens, your dreams start falling into place. All things start with self-love and self-acceptance. If we treat ourselves with dignity, compassion, kindness, and love then we are more likely to treat others that way and create a world around us which reflects that.

Chapter 4 Rewind

Once the practice of self-love is expanded, we see more clearly the people around us and our connection with them. What did you discover in the "Journey to Connection"? Do you struggle with certain relationships more or less than you realized? As you've gotten older have you chosen people with similar values and personality traits or really changed it up because you are changing?

How you interact with other people can be a blessing . . . or a curse. You need patience, thoughtfulness, and openness when you engage with another human. Every hour, day, week, and year, we leave a trail of interactions behind us like the wake of a boat. What does your wake look like? Are you proud of it? At peace with it? There are so many levels to interactions, but they can all have an impact. Someone you are in line with at the grocery store or at the gas station, your best friend or your significant other are all different levels of interactions. Do you work on making them all positive? Is your cake a beautiful rainbow with sparkles on top or is it a chunky, muddy poo fest? There will be days when it's one or the other. That's okay, but overall, what do we want to strive for?

Chapter 5 Rewind

As you moved along in this book, you moved from looking at how you interact from a personal standpoint to looking at who you choose to have around you. The people you share values, interests, and passions with. You looked at your strengths and how you can bring people and your beloved personal icons into your life to help support and inspire you in Chapter 5. Your warrior soul is strengthened by those you have around you.

Chapter 6 Rewind

You have identified and investigated your north star. You know what your spiritual path looks like and where you want it to take you. What part will it play in setting your goals and achieving your dreams? Have you developed any new spiritual practices in working towards your north star? Have you changed anything about how you connect with spirit?

DAILY PRACTICE AND INTENTION

The more you connect with your spirit and engage in practices that support heart-centered living and connection, the more you will stay engaged with your true self. The best way to do that is through daily practice. That practice can be very simple. Pick a few things that are most important to you and try to incorporate them into your life. Meditation, breath-work, prayer, nature walks, and journaling are all simple ways you can incorporate connection with your spirit into your life.

Awareness can help you incorporate all the things we have covered in SPARK!. Take notice of how you are responding to various situations, how you are being treated, and how you are treating others.

RESOURCES AND FOLLOW-UPS

We are reaching the end of this book, but your journey is just beginning. I want to share with you a few resources and places you will find support for this book. There are lots of things happening at mysparkjourney.com. You can work along with me as I complete the creative activities at the end of each chapter or deep dive into any area of this book that you want more information on.

There will be links to videos on the YouTube channel, SPARK!-Soul Therapy. There is an online meditation room, a music box with playlists to enjoy on Apple Music and Spotify, and many other inspirational bits and pieces to support the changes you have made on this journey.

Life is an incredible expedition into the unknown. You learn as you go. Exploring all the crazy cracks and crevices of the universe can guide, inspire, and nurture your spark as it bursts forth from your dreaming, curious, creative, wise, incredible self.

I encourage you to keep using all the things discovered in this book to keep fanning the flames of your life and your dreams. Here is your chance to ignite your unique, precious spark and light the whole world!

Welcome to the universe within, welcome to your SPARK!, welcome home!
Your journey is just beginning.

Resources

QR Code

BONUS BOOK CONTENT

Because you have purchased Spark! you have access to exclusive content to help you on your journey!

Scan the QR code on this page for access to all the extra goodies.

Resources

Videos & Connection

Check out my YouTube channel where I have videos about building and "blinging" your tool kit. Plus, on the website there's a downloadable version for purchase with extra blinging and writing space. Then come connect with me on social meda and tell me about your experience.

- ♥ Instagram: mysparkjourney
- ♥ X: mysparkjourney
- ♥ Facebook: My Spark Journey
- ♥ YouTube: Spark!-Soul Therapy

FURTHER READING

- Albrecht, K. (2007) *Practical Intelligence: The Art and Science of Common Sense.* San Francisco: Jossy-Bass Publishers.

- Erikson, E.H. (1980) *Identity and the Life Cycle.* NY: Norton and Company Publishers, Inc.

- Williamson, M. (1993) *A Return To Love: Reflections on the Principles of A Course in Miracles.* NY: HarperCollins Publishers, Inc.

About Gale

I'm Gale! I'm a Clinical Social Worker and Therapist. I have worked with young women in all stages of growth and transition for over a decade. OK, probably closer to two decades, lol!! I've worked in schools, community settings, mental health settings and private practice.

I have met so many incredible women, in all stages of life and growth, over the years. These women have been "coming into themselves" and looking to discover all the magic and mysteries about themselves and the world around them. I realized that it would be awesome if there was a place where there were more opportunities for inspiration, fun, joy, creativity, relaxation, self-exploration, and other things to bring inspiration into all our lives.

I created a space where women can focus on themselves and feel supported. A place where there is healing, joy, creativity, and ideas without judgment.

That place is Spark, both the book and the website. I hope you've enjoyed the book and I hope you will come and visit me on the website. Meanwhile, my warmest wishes to you on your journey. Best of luck. You got this!

WWW.MYSPARKJOURNEY.COM

*Never forget.
You are stardust.*

www.ingramcontent.com/pod-product-compliance
Lightning Source LLC
Chambersburg PA
CBHW080346170426
43194CB00014B/2697